Pride of the Nation

Sardar Patel

Renu Saran

DIAMOND BOOKS

Publisher : **Diamond Pocket Books (P) Ltd.**
X-30, Okhla Industrial Area, Phase-II
New Delhi-110020
Phone : 011-40712200
E-mail : sales@dpb.in
Website : www.dpb.in
Printed by : Repro (India)

Sardar Patel

By - *Renu Saran*

Publisher's Note

Those who leave their imprint upon people's heart could be divided into two categories. One category is of those who do win people's hearts but their imprint doesn't last long as with the passage of time it fades. The other category is of those who not only win people's hearts during their life-time but with the passage of time their popularity grows even more. People often remember them saying that things would have been different had they been alive! In other words, they transcend time and become immortal. Because what they do in their life-time meets not only the contemporary needs but even in future its relevance remains unmitigated. Their deeds naturally appeal the hearts of the people. Their imprint remains indelible. Sardar Vallabh Bhai Patel belongs to this second category. Whatever he did right during the freedom movement to country's independence was for ensuring welfare of not only common man, society and the nation but even of the coming generations as well. His deeds also remained a beacon for the Gen-next. Owing to his iron-will, steely resolves and indomitable courage, he earned the epithet: 'The Iron Man' which truly reflected his personality. He had all these qualities: housing a human heart in the iron frame. When a practicing lawyer, his arguments would convince the most headstrong judges and during the freedom movement he would outwit even the most cunning British officers. It was his single-minded commitment that could unite a country divided into hundreds of kingdoms into one robust nation. His style of governance in the maintenance of law and order still appears the ideal way to ensure progress of the nation. Even in the context of creating an ideal India his whole life appears to be a planned philosophy. Despite all these qualities, it is sheerly ironical that owing to the modern day political manipulations, the government documents recognized his dynamic approach and evolutionary philosophy quite belatedly. With the result he got his due honour after a long lapse though he deserved it immediately after India's independence. This act does reflect poorly on the thinking of the Administration of that time when much less deserving leaders jumped the queue for the most coveted 'Bharat Ratna' award. Not only that, some even received it during their life-time itself.

Nevertheless, there is definitely something in this name: Sardar Patel, so mesmerizing that the emergence of it diffuses all opposition instantly and the people start saying: "only if Sardar Patel be alive to-day!" While one group of people blames the present Administration for going astray from the ideals set by him, yet another longs for his presence to feel satisfied with whatever the progress the country has made thus far. All told, Sardar Patel's name is worth the reverence from every group.

Come, let us recollect the various aspects of his life which were not only practical and implementable but satisfied the emotional or sensitive needs of the era as well. Patriotism was the part of his inheritance. His father Jhaver Bhai ardently supported the freedom agitations and hoped to see his next generation equally active in these movements. He longed to have someone in his family or at least in his village who could help unleash the chains of slavery tying Mother India. And his this wish was comprehensively fulfilled. Born in October 1875, Sardar Patel not only fulfilled his wish but even exceeded that. His achievements made everyone proud not only in his family or village but in the entire region. Sardar Patel was a born leader. During his schooling days, the teachers then paid greater emphasis on selling the books rather than teaching them. And his reaction to this system was: 'how would purity of education survive if the teacher becomes a trader?' His views about the law of the land were very humane. He believed that: "Laws are made for men and hence their implementing officers and the judges who give their verdict must have humanistic view point. Their conviction in human welfare must be equally strong."

At this juncture, his wife deserves a hallowed mention who contributed evenly in his efforts. Notwithstanding God calling her back rather too soon, the flame for being the front-runner kindled by her inspired him all through his life. That is why, our revered Sardar is still adorable and worthy of all reverence. One of his most desirable qualities is his service to humanity, reflected in the time of 'Godhra Plague'. Vallabh Bhai enthusiastically participated in the social activities and boldly showed his firm stand in the cultural and religious disputes that kept on surfacing during that period. But if we judge the 'equality to all religious concept' in the present perspective we may say that his ideas have not yet been vindicated. On the contrary, the concept has been progressively polluted. His views expressed then on the sham religious practices appear very much relevant even now. With reference to a religious priest, Maharaj Ji, his view was: "All right Sire! But if I find Maharaj Ji to be the culprit, I may plead his case but can't go against law…!"

His this one statement conclusively proves that the law of the land took the precedence over his love for the family. In fact his views were very practical and realistic. At one point he asserts: "A religious head of a shrine can't become a deity himself!"

Even a hundred years ago he never considered any priest above the law. Now when the so called Saints and Saadhus get exposed about their involvement in the vile practices, his far-sightedness appears very much relevant.

What deserves repeated reference is the bitter fact that we couldn't give him as much honour as to make him revered forever as the public leader. We don't say that his popularity is less but only if the governmental agencies had spread his thoughts and views in public through the audio-visual media, perhaps today his name would have been on the tongues of every children in all the urban and rural sectors. Regrettably his very ideals that we use while defining the phases of progress appear to have been sidetracked when we seek his wide popularity. But more baffling is the fact that when someone tries to make him recognized as one of the luminaries of the world and install his statue at the highest pedestal in the world, either the effort is politicized with the tainted glasses or is derided in the social context! Why must this happen? Why can't we accept this noble work with complete dedication and faith that it deserves? Perhaps privately all accept it this way but they feel shy in confessing it publicly! Why should we put 'ifs and buts' in installing his tallest statue who made us hold our heads high in pride by his dedicated acts during and after the freedom struggle?

Let us now have some plain talks! Our Prime Minister Shri Narendra Modi's endeavour to have the grand statue of Sardar Patel installed should be supported by all in unison. He who is devoted to accomplishing this noble endeavour also deserves our uninhibited praise because such noble acts are neither ever censured or opposed but only lauded. Since Sardar Patel was the 'Iron-Man', his statue must also be as strong as steel! Secondly, he is a popular national leader and hence people of the entire nation must participate the installation of his statue.

Here it must be clarified that Sardar Patel never hankered after any award or praise or honour. Equally true is the fact that no award or honour can ever cover his grand personality but does it not behove us to do something for our leader who made India stand with pride in the entire world? Shouldn't we do something to attract global attention and make the world look at it with respect? If this pious endeavour is viewed with politicalized glasses, it is our sheer misfortune! Sardar Patel never sought importance and honour for himself. He kept on blooming like a flower with the fragrance of his penance and sacrifice kept on spreading all around. The famous poem: "Ek Phool Ki Chaah" (The desire of a flower) has the following lines, as though written to sum up his wish as well:

"I don't want to be laced as an ornament
in the divine-dame's décor;
Pluck me off O Gardner!
And throw me on the path,
Treaded by the brave to save
the honour of their Motherland!"

Now let us learn greater details about the installation of Sardar Patel's that grand Statue.

The 'Rashtriya Ekta Parishad' convened under the chairmanship of Shri Narendra Modi, has decided to install a huge iron statue of Sardar Vallabh Bhai Patel, popularly called the 'Iron-Man' the world over, at the bank of the Narmada River's Sarovar Dam. With the expected height of 597.1 feet, this is likely to be the tallest statue of the world. It has also been decided to seek 1 kg iron and 100 gms of soil from every village and the work for collection of the iron and soil has already been started. As the representative from every village, the photograph of every 'Gram-Pradhan' shall also be collected in this unique campaign. The soil mentioned here will be collected from the fields of every village.

Collection of iron and soil for making this statue is very apt in this context as Sardar Patel was normally renowned as the 'Iron-Man'. His steely resolves and principles made even the mighty British cower in his dominance. Hence the whole nation must participate in having his iron statue installed on the highest pedestal. Since Sardar Patel had special love for the farmers and the soil of our country, it is an eminently proper proposal to include the soil of the nation in his grand statue's making. Perhaps his message to the countrymen was summed up in the following couplet as he could never compromise with his self-respect and love for his country.

Jisko na nij gaurav tatha nij desh par abhimaan hai!
Wah nar nahin nar-pashu niraa hai aur mritak samaan hai!!

(He who has no respect and pride for his country is not human but an animal, a dead-load on the earth.)

Let us learn some of his rare qualities which justify the popular title he is known by: the 'Iron Man'.

Even after receiving the telegram announcing his wife's death he was not distracted from his work and even decided not to read the message, showing the commitment for his work and the great capacity of his heart to tolerate personal tragedy.

At that time, when the lawyers cowered in opening their mouth before the English Magistrates, Sardar Patel would, undauntedly, plead his client's case in his stentorian voice. Just read this episode:

'Vallabh Patel said in a louder voice: "Please have this glass removed from here." The audience was amazed because nobody could dare speak in such a powerful voice in that court.'

This episode highlights his fearlessness. Even in pleading the most serious cases his logic power never diminished. In a rape case he was willing to plead not from the victim's side but from the rapist side. But behind this decision stood his sensitive and soft feelings for womankind. In this context he said: "In order to ensure the girl's honour not getting hampered in the court before all, I may be forced to plead from the rapist's side."

No matter what the circumstances be, Vallabh Bhai knew how to be firm on his stand; though at times either he would force the circumstances toe his line or he would adjust his stand to act according to the conditions prevailing then. All these details repeatedly raise the same question: Why our resolve to honour globally this man of firm principles, very much worldliwise, so well endowed with power of logic, having an impressive personality, capable of attracting people like a powerful magnet, saviour of the farmers and so self-respecting patriot, should be politicized with tainted interpretations?

It is a well-known fact that Sardar Patel was deeply hurt with the assassination of Mahatma Gandhi. This was the reason why he condemned this act of Nathuram Godse who murdered Gandhi Ji and himself banned the Rashtriya Swayam Sewak Sangh (RSS) as Godse had connection with this organization. It is interesting to note that the resolve to install the tallest statue of Sardar Patel, was initiated by Narendra Modi who himself has connections with the RSS, which caused much flutter in the political galleries.

It is quite natural that the one who banned your Sangh and your resolve to start a campaign to make him a global celebrity do raise many question marks. However, the reality is not what it appears to be. If viewed from another angle it is clear that there is hardly any room for the feeling of selection, rejection, ban and prohibition to surface in this noble gesture. What Mr. Modi wants is to give the Iron-Man globally a tall stature for his unparallel achievement of merging 552 kingdoms and handing us India as a united nation. It is altogether a different issue that for the sake of proper governance we let that nation emerge as a federal state with 29 states and 7 union territories. Going by the opinion of various statesmen it is a global truth that decentralization of power strengthens the relation between the ruler and the ruled and ensures better prosperity and self-defence. Here the basic fact shouldn't be missed that no matter how many states we create, no state can ever be above India as a nation. All the states are the inalienable units of the Indian Federation and no unit can be bigger than the whole nation. We have to create an India which has unity in diversity. Mr. Modi's dream is 'One India: Best India'. His this vision matches well with what Sardar Patel had dreamt for India.

When in the national, public and social interest two streams of thoughts merge, there remains no room for any opposition; no scope for political manipulations or prejudices. Another major point in this context is that, later on, Sardar Patel himself did recognize the Sangh (RSS) again. Its direct inference is that a disturbance created due to special conditions can't be painted as the reason for ever-lasting animosity. Had the temporary disturbance between the Sangh and Patel gone deeper into Sangh's heart, then it would have also adversely affected Modi's popularity. But nothing of the sort has happened.

With this detailed analysis of the various situations, at least this much should be a foregone conclusion that we must feel proud to participate in the installation of the Grand Statue of Sardar Patel, the glaring symbol of Modi's concept: "One India: Best India'; that we all must enthusiastically join this campaign owing to its national fervour. Instead of making it a political issue out of vested interest, we must deem it to be an issue of national glory and hence we ought to honour the person committed to the resolve of enhancing India's pride.

He whose vision of unity in diversity
Has added to India's pride;
He who makes India stand united on the global screen;
Come! We must offer our flowers of faith
With the bowed heads –
On his dream of installing a grand statue of our Iron-Man
With a commitment of total participation.

– Narendra Kumar Verma

Sardar Patel

The sky was covered with clouds of various colours – dark, red, yellow, with an occasional white cloud passing through them as through a sheepish smile flitting across the face of a grief stricken person. The sky also thundered with roar of the collision of oppositely charged cloud-layers like the echoing of the footfalls of the person walking on a footway below on earth. A twenty year old youth, with a resolve to do something extraordinary, was moving with firm steps, determined to find a highway of some excellence in his life. His foot struck against a pebble obstructing his way. He bent down, lifted the pebble and threw it far away as removing an obstruction of his way.

The youth suddenly realized that his native village, Karamsad, was now far behind as though the entire area of his ten acre land now stood squeezed in the footway he was treading on, as though his entire *Taluka* (land-hold) stood lost in the trees of the jungle bordering Borsad. Long ago he had heard a Sadhu saying that one had to lose a small piece of land to get a huge farm and in life too, minor sacrifices often resulted in major achievements.

All of a sudden he stopped, detecting a movement closely, amidst the dense trees and shrub. A shadowy figure appeared to approach him. He became alert and stared ahead: a man of 40-45, came closer with his left hand pressing the hurt portion of his right hand. The pain of the wound was reflecting upon that stranger's face. The youth asked the stranger: "Who are you, Bhai?"

"I… I'm Bhushan Rao… and you?"

"My name is Jhaver Patel and I'm from Gujarat."

"What a fine coincidence that we two from neighbouring states meeting at this place suddenly."

"The whole life is a series of coincidences. Who meets whom, where and why – all are coincidences."

Jhaver had seen that Bhushan's wound was oozing blood. He quickly tore a piece of the cloth from the end part of his *Gamacha* (a hanky-type piece of cloth kept on the shoulder) and tied it around the wound on Bhushan's hand. Now both started moving on the foot-walk.

"Where to?" Bhushan asked.

"To get recruited in the army of Rani-Jhansi (Queen of Jhansi)."

"Really?"

"And you? Where from… and this wound and blood?"

"Coming exactly from where you are heading to."

"What?"

"I'm also a soldier in Rani Jhansi's army, young man! We were preparing for a big onslaught but a minor confrontation occurred and I was hit by an arrow in that."

"Now where you're planning to go?"

"Close by the end of this footwalk dwells a Haqueem (Unani doctor) known to me, for getting this wound properly dressed by him."

Both went to the nearby Haqueem. After dressing the wound, they started their journey towards army centre of Rani of Jhansi. On the way, Bhushan told Jhaver many things about Rani Lakshmibai (of Jhansi) and Nana Saheb. He informed Jhaver that Rani Ji was planning a big fight against the British, the first major step to get over the British dominance.

They traveled for long exchanging views and Bhushan giving him a lot of information.

Bhushan's narration of war preparations against the British inspired Jhaver more. He developed a kind of spring in his feet. Bhushan also walked fast with him forgetting his aching wound, as if both wanted to reach the army recruitment centre of Nana Saheb in no time.

During this phase Bhushan also told about the minor knights and small Talukdars or Zamindars who deemed themselves quite influential and were sychophants of the British, totally indifferent to this war of independence.

At last they reached the recruitment centre. Bhushan introduced Jhaver to Sadashiv Holkar, a lieutenant in that army preparing his squad for the big confrontation. Soon the preparations were over and he informed Nana Saheb about his squad's readiness.

Meanwhile, Rani Lakshmi Bai and Nana Saheb had made themselves ready for the struggle for independence. The British were trying their best to seize Rani's forces and she was also willing to have an armed confrontation with them.

However, despite all the preparations an explosion before the decided moment turned all their plans and the Rani had to face defeat. Leaving all his wounded soldiers she breathed her last and became a martyr.

The news of her death diffused her forces and they ran helter-skelter. Jhaver also found him among the captive soldiers arrested for associating with Malhar Rao Holkar who fought against the British.

When released later on, the young-man Jhaver was quite confused: whether the war fought by Rani Jhansi and others was just a failed mutiny against the British or it was the first war for India's independence! 'Be whatever it be', he thought, 'this much is certain that now this flame kindled by our revered Rani-Jhansi and Nana Saheb will not be doused till we achieve total redemption from the foreign rule.'

With these thoughts in his mind, he returned to his native village from Indore where he stayed for some time. Returning home he always wished in his mind: 'Only if we could have someone in our family or at least in our village who may snap the chains tying our motherland in the domination of the foreigners. O God! please fulfill my wish!'

And as if God was waiting to answer his prayers! When he got married he had three sons. When his wife Lad Bai was pregnant for the fourth time, he found his dreams invariably showing the scenes of his participation in the war against the foreigners, fought about almost two decades back.

On 31st October 1875, his house reverberated with the songs sung at the time of a male child's birth. His fourth son, to be called Vallabh on account of the child's robust physique, was born to fulfill his ardent wish that he sought from God years ago. Eventually this boy, Vallabh, was born to liberate the motherland from the foreign yoke.

Jhaver Bhai was a man of limited means. Surviving on the produce from his meagre land he wanted his sons to become educated. While helping their father in their free time, they were admitted to a primary school in Petlad. A teacher in that school, who detected a streak of brilliance in Jhaver's youngest son, Vallabh, asked Jhaver not to waste his son's brilliance in the farming. So he had Vallabh admitted to a secondary school in nearby Nadiad. It was in this phase of his education that Vallabh's basic traits were revealed. A born leader, he was courageous and could never tolerate any practice appearing unethical to him.

Unfortunately the teachers in that Nadiad school acted more as the traders than as the teachers. They would buy all the course books from the publishers at a low rate and make their students buy at high rates. Vallabh protested against this wrong practice. Vallabh got all support from his fellow students and became their leader. They stopped going to class and resorted to a mild form of strike. The parents also supported their wards. The school had to remain closed for some days. Eventually the teachers had to bow and this practice was stopped. But even after having defeated the teachers on this point, Vallabh continued to show respect to them. This was a peculiar trait of his personality, which was seen in his actions all through his life. He was never vindictive. Once the cause of the dissension was removed, he would be just normal with his opponents.

For further studies, Vallabh had to go to Baroda (Vadodara) and got admitted in a matric school. But here he had to face another confrontation with his Gujarati teacher. The students there had to choose one of the languages and Vallabh chose his mother tongue, Gujarati. Although his Gujarati teacher, Chhote Lal Ji, taught this language, he had great love for Sanskrit and wanted most of the students should choose Sanskrit.

Once the teacher summoned Vallabh to the staff-room and asked:

"Where are you from?" He asked sternly.

"From Nadiad," replied Vallabh.

"So you prefer Gujarati? Why not Sanskrit?"

"My mother tongue is Gujarati. I want to acquire good command over it before learning any other language."

"But, don't you realize that Sanskrit is the mother of all languages including Gujarati?"

Vallabh now realized the teacher's love for Sanskrit. He argued: "Sir! If we don't learn Gujarati, whom you will teach?"

Such an argumentative answer with a hiding question was not expected from an adolescent! The teacher suddenly got angry. In order to punish Vallabh for his open defiance, the teacher asked Vallabh to stand on the bench. Vallabh's fellow students also found it rather objectionable. But the teacher was still not satisfied. He asked Vallabh to write all the tables and show him every day. This was adding insult to injury: asking a matric students to write tables! The collective objection of the students was reported to the Head Master. While the Head Master was probing the matter, he received yet another complaint from Chhote Lal Ji that Vallabh was not obeying his orders. Vallabh did write the tables a few days and then stopped doing so on the plea: "the tables have run away!" The teacher felt insulted and told the Head Master about it. Vallabh was summoned by him. Upon further enquiry Vallabh said: "Sir, this is an exercise in futility. Had he asked me to write something from our lesson, I would have learnt something. Writing tables is just a trick to humiliate me. So I refused."

The Head Master saw the sense in Vallabh's argument and let him go. But about two months later Vallabh again had a tiff with yet another teacher. Helpless by his nature, he couldn't compromise with anything not proper according to his logic. So in 1897 he had to back-track to Nadiad and there he cleared his Matriculate Examination at the age of 22. Now Vallabh was on the threshold of his active life; the stage had come when he had to choose his vocation. Vallabh wanted to go to England for higher education in the legal field but his family could not afford him for this course. Then his family members advised him to clear the 'Mukhtari' course which he cleared easily. He started to do his legal practice in Godhra. He soon became famous for his clear-headedness and his courage to face the English Magistrates undauntedly. At that time, bowing before the Englishmen was the norm of the day but Vallabh transcended this rule.

Once the Magistrate told him in a stern voice when he was pleading a case: "Perhaps you're not aware that it is a criminal case."

"No Sir! I know it well," countered young Vallabh, "and that is why I have not only brought the written documents but also the live witness." He won that case. His logical reasoning, powerful voice and insight into the human psyche made him win his cases in a row. In no time his fame as a lawyer spread far and wide. His chamber began to have the unending queue of the clients willing to engage him for their cases. Apart from his comprehensive legal knowledge, strong pleas and the rarest presence of mind, his basically humane approach to all the cases made him the favourite of his clients. He also believed that not only the lawyer but also the judge must never forget that they deal with humans and not with machines or animals.

Success in legal practice in Godhra made him somewhat affluent. By this time he had already been the father of a daughter, 'Maniben', who was playing on his lap. After some time he got a son named 'Dahya Bhai'. Life was quite comfortable. His wife, Jhaverba was a very devoted wife and a very methodical lady. Her managing the household affairs well, gave Vallabh much time to enhance his legal practice. Now he had a thought of going to a bigger city like Baroda or Ahmedabad. But before he could take any step in that direction, deadly plague engulfed Godhra. This epidemic made many quit that town. Patel was also advised to quit the place but he had his commitment to his clients; his cases were still pending. Unless the court closed he couldn't have left Godhra!

So he wanted his wife and kids to leave Godhra immediately.

"You should leave for Karamsad immediately."

"No! I can't leave you here alone."

"I say you must go. Plague is spreading here fast."

"You could also come in its strike range!"

"Nothing will happen to me."

"How can you say so. Aren't you human?"

Vallabh knew Jhaverba's nature. She could do anything but not leave her husband this way. He remembered her stubbornness when he was planning to take up the Mukhtar course. Most of his family men were skeptical about his completing this course successfully. It was only his wife who gave him courage. When the question emerged as to where he should go for legal practice, his father wanted him to go and work with his elder brother, Vitthal. But Jhaverba was against it. She wanted him to do so on his own strength. At last, Vallabh agreed to her proposal and decided to work in Godhra. Now when the question emerged Jhaverba's leaving Godhra, Patel reminded her: "At that time, I had bowed before your insistence. Now you must listen to me."

At last Jhaverba agreed to leave Godhra as Vallabh wanted and left for Karmsad with kids, though she was still worried for her husband's health. And what she was fearing actually happened. Vallabh was afflicted with this deadly disease. But timely treatment soon made him recover fully.

Meanwhile, reaching Karamsad, Jhaverba herself fell ill. Hearing about her illness Vallabh was quite perturbed. He was missing her. Often he would recollect the days when they were together. He remembered a past incident.

It was the beginning of his practice. One day he returned from work quite exhausted. Financially they were quite hard-pressed. When his wife offered him some milk and snacks, he was surprised.

He asked: "From where you procured these things?"

She insisted: "First you must eat these and drink milk. You'll feel quite refreshed. It is necessary for you to have a healthy diet."

Vallabh: "It is okay. But you must tell how you arranged these things."

"No, first you must have these!"

"All right," said Vallabh and ate the snacks and drank milk, and then asked: "Now tell me. How did you get these things?"

"If I reveal, promise that you won't admonish me," she said meekly.

"Did I ever say a harsh word to you?"

"Okay! You know many uneducated girls dwell around. They know nothing. Not even good songs!" Jhaverba said.

"This isn't the answer to my query. Come to the point." Vallabh said rather irritatingly.

Now Jhaverba came closer. Holding a button of Vallabh's kurta affectionately, she said: "Now listen patiently. You know five or six girls of our neighbourhood got married recently. Many of them want to write letters to their spouse but they don't know how to write. One day I was just humming a song, three / four of them came to me and made me sing the full song at their request. They loved it. Then one of them asked shyly: "Do you also know how to write?"

I said: "Yes! Of course I can write!" Whereupon one of them requested me to write a letter to her husband as dictated by her. I did so. And then she brought some edibles out of pure gratitude. This way I get these things. I write letters and they give me these things. Did I do anything wrong?"

"No!" said Vallabh. "But which song did you sing?"

"The same which I sang before you just after my marriage: *Koel baithee hai more, O bane omli je, Boliya O vachan suhaavanaa je...!"*

Vallabh made Jhaverba sing this song fully. After a moment he asked:

"Do the girls pay you for writing letters in cash or kind?"

"Not in cash! I don't sell my knowledge! I accept these things – milk, cream or sweets out of their gratitude. At times they offer fresh vegetables from their farm."

Vallabh said: "I never knew about your these abilities. It is all okay. I also believe that apart from doing the household jobs, the young girls must be literate. They also deserve knowledge to prove their worth apart from their utility.

Suddenly some plague afflicted persons' whimpers bought him to the bitter present. People, animals – all were dying. Rotten dead rats were being found in all houses. He became busy in getting medicines for the patients and arranging funerals for dead persons.

While the plague panic was subsiding, there arose a problem about two temple's ownership. Vallabh's family priest was also drawn in this dispute. His father wanted his 'Maharaj Ji' to be favoured as the case was with Vallabh only. Vallabh told his father frankly, "I will continue fighting for the Maharaj Ji but if I found him guilty in any way, then I'll let the law take its own course."

Jhaver Patel (his father) said: "No, Maharaj Ji can't be guilty. He is a pious man… a saint."

"Nobody becomes pious like God by staying in a God's temple," replied Vallabh.

"But our own man deserves protection," the father was still insisting with a paternal authority.

Vallabh thought for a moment and said with courage: "I will side with truth, come what may!"

Vallabh had to face such emotional storms many a time. Even in his professional field he had to encounter many difficulties.

Once he had a case in an English Magistrate's court who was very arrogant and foul-tongued. He would use any derogatory language for anyone. Knowing about Patel appearing before that foul-tongued Judge, many of his fellow lawyers, who nursed a kind of jealousy for Vallabh's spectacular rise, were very keen to see the outcome of that day's proceedings.

When Vallabh was getting ready for going to the court, his assistant came to him with the file and said: "Sir! Today is our day of the fire-test. Many other lawyers are expecting that you'd have a very gruelling day."

"Let them expect whatever they like. Let us go to the court." Vallabh replied his assistant and went to the court.

As soon as the judge occupied his seat, there was complete silence. All were afraid, lest the judge should show his violent temper. But Vallabh was very calm and balanced.

That was the day when witnesses had to be questioned. As one witness was called in, Vallabh said in his loud voice: "Please have that mirror removed." All the persons present there were amazed, 'such a loud instruction before the judge, Mr. Husbond!' The judge questioned his logic about the removal of the mirror and refused to have that mirror removed. Then Patel said in a 'tongue in cheek' manner. "Then my witness would speak with his face turned the other way from the mirror." The Magistrate was baffled but there was no rule under which he could force the witness give his statements facing the mirror.

Other lawyers were amazed. "He is really a genius and courageous as well."

"I hope he'll go far up. May he become a Judge or Magistrate himself."

But some one said, "His wisdom will be better utilized in politics. The country needs such brilliant person!"

Similarly, all were surprised when Vallabh was approached by his close friend for fighting a rape case. He asked: "Such maddening cases also come here?"

"They do. There is no limit to man's depravity which can show its ugly face anywhere."

"So, what do you want me to do?" Vallabh asked.

"I want that girl's honour remain secured."

"Then I'd plead from the rapist side."

"What?"

"Because should I plead from the victim's side, then I'd ask such searching questions that the dirtiest linen would get washed in public!"

Bewildered the close friend walked away.

In fact Vallabh's original interpretation of various laws and their applications gave him a unique position in the law courts. He would, by his perfect arguments based on the human psychology, win even such cases as were declared 'gone cases' by his fellow lawyers. He would make his witness pose some quite unanswerable questions to silence the other party. At times his fellow lawyers would come to him to learn the very approach towards their cases and consult about the way of presenting them before the judges. Many English judges also found his arguments irrefutable. Things were looking quite nosy in the professional field. His reputation had also made him quite popular. Many social organizations would invite him to their functions. He had developed a leaning towards the 'Arya Samaj Movement' which had become quite popular in Gujarat. Vallabh was also convinced that the false and misguided interpretations of the religious texts had caused many social ills, which was also the basic belief of the Arya Samaj.

In the meantime, his fame spread far and wide as much as to make a British company offer him a trip to England for doing the bar-at-law course. It was a quite lucrative offer as all promising lawyers wished it. His elder brother Vitthal was also willing to do it. Although Vallabh was quite willing to go, detecting his elder brother's this wish, he suggested him to go instead. Since the ticket was for V. J. Patel (for Vallabh Jhaver Patel) he suggested Vitthal to go as V. J. Patel (Vitthal Jhaver Patel) also suited his name. Further, there was no photograph to be fixed on the ticket. Also their age difference was negligible. Vallabh's this sacrifice ever remained etched on Vitthal's memory. This way Vallabh made his elder brother go to England for this most coveted course. Vitthal was overwhelmed with gratitude for his younger brother's this sacrifice.

***

Vallabh busied himself in his practice after the departure of his wife to Karamsad. Although professionally he was doing well, soon he was to face a major emotional upheaval.

His wife's prolonged illness revealed her having a tumour in her stomach. When Vallabh went to his native village to see his sick wife, the doctor suggested operation immediately. Jhaverba was unwilling to go to Bombay for this purpose. She was afraid of getting admitted to a hospital. But Vallabh explained: "This hospital in Bombay has many competent doctors. I will keep on visiting you, there. Bombay is not far off. You will have many well-wishers to look after you."

Vallabh went back to his work sending his wife to that hospital in Bombay. In Godhra many cases were pending and he could not frequently go to Bombay. The operation was done but Jhaverba couldn't survive. Although Vallabh had some misgivings he was too tied in his work. One day while he was busy pleading his case, a telegramme was received. He continued pleading the case after keeping the telegramme in his pocket. In the evening when the court time was over, some of his friends reminded him about the telegramme: "You didn't even open the envelop to read the telegramme." Vallabh said with a grief stricken face: "There is no need to open it. I know, my wife has expired!"

His friends were bewildered to see his capacity to absorb such an emotional trauma so nonchalantly. Vallabh was heart-broken but he continued his work. He had to look after his clients' welfare, which he couldn't have sacrificed at the altar of his personal tragedy. He confided his feelings in one of his close friend, Mr. Desai. "There is no sense in crying over the inevitable. If such was God's will, could my wailing over my wife's most untimely demise have brought her back to life? And in the consequence my clients' interest would have suffered. Why to feel sorry about the past that has already been passed?"

Although he had said it, Jhaverba's memory did hurt him in his loneliness. Repeatedly her favourite song: "*Koel baithee hai…*" echoed in his quiet nights.

***

When Jhaverba died, Vallabh was hardly 34. He was pressurized to remarry but he refused. Of course he was worried for his children's upbringing but he found an able support in the form of Vitthal Bhai who was leading a settled life in Bombay. Vitthal was now back as the bar-at-law and he voluntarily took the responsibility of rearing up Mani and Dahya.

Vallabh immersed himself in his work with a doubled intensity for he found the best way to overcome his wife's memory was to keep his mind engaged in his work. At time he would go to Bombay to ensure his motherless children. Although Vitthal's wife was very miser yet Vitthal ensured his wife's no activity obstructed Vallabha's progeny's happy dwelling in Bombay.

As his luck would have it, soon Vallabh got an opportunity to go to England and fulfill his long coveted wish: getting the degree of bar-at-law. In 1910 August he received a message from the famous college: 'Middle Temple' that his admission had been granted.

He prepared to leave for England. Since he was still not affluent, he had to arrange funds for his England visit. But he was worried about his children's education. Fortunately, due to the contacts of an English lady, Ms. Wilson his children were admitted to the Saint Marry's School. That lady also assured him that she would act as their local guardian. Now everything was duly arranged and Vallabh reached the port to take up a long voyage to England by the sea route.

As he reached the ship and observed the arrangements, he found one problem. There appeared not much edibles on the ship for the vegetarians. But before having any appetite he had to face another problem: sea-sickness. On the dock he met the doctor of the ship who suggested: "Mr. Patel! You must alter your dietary pattern. Turn non-vegetarian during this sea-journey."

"No doctor! This is impossible."

"When the question of survival comes, many turn non-veg. This is the question of life and death."

"One can find many arguments for turning non-veg. But, doctor, it is not only a case of taste or faith for me. I can't eat anything prepared after killing a live body."

This way not only that Indian doctor but many other fellow passengers advised Vallabh to have meat to overcome the problem of the sea-sickness. There was a lady, Madam Safrania who even advised Vallabh to drink a little alcohol.

"Then you'll find the non-veg dishes particularly tasty."

But Vallabh stuck to his guns. His indomitable will was unlikely to break no matter what the people did. Surviving on the frugal diet of fruits, vegetables and bread, he at last reached England. No doubt the cold climate there made him shiver under his insufficient clothes, he was happy to have reached England with his body and soul still together.

While he was still acclimatizing himself standing on the port and observing the cold and damp atmosphere all around, the doctor, who was with him in the journey, addressed him:

"Oh, Mr. Patel! You're still here!"

"Yes! I'm trying to find the best way to go to my destination!"

"And what is it?"

"The Middle Temple College. I got my admission in that famous institution."

The doctor said with a smile: "I can take you there. It is on my way!"

"Why should you bother?" Vallabh was unwilling to trouble the doctor.

"Oh! It isn't a matter of bother for me! Rather it's my pleasure to help the one who survived the sea voyage on the strength of his principles," the doctor added with a glint in his eyes.

By that time a car came to take the doctor to his place. He dropped Vallabh at his desired destination.

Vallabh found everything new and strange there. "I have to pass three years here in this strange environment," he reminded himself.

Vallabh met the concerned officer of the institution, Mr. Cook, who appeared to be a nice gentleman. Mr. Cook not only told him about the college and the surrounding places, but also made him meet Mrs. Margaret. She willingly let out an airy, clean room for his stay. She also offered him a sumptuous breakfast. Vallabh found her to be a well read cultured woman who knew much about Indian customs and culture; and had much respect for India as well. He thanked his stars for this coincidence: getting a very helpful doctor and a very accommodating land-lady! Although Vallabh had all through a man of action yet now he realized that destiny did have its own say. Problems kept on arising for last couple of years but his destiny gave him a convenient way to overcome that. With two minor kids to take care after his wife's most unexpected and untimely death, he had an affectionate elder brother to make him sail through that emotional storm rather unscathed! A journey to a foreign country and he got much help from the doctor and now such a considerate lady to ensure his comfortable stay in England. Mrs. Margaret's knowledge about the Indian history – particularly about Chanakya – the ancient wizard in the state-craft – really baffled Vallabh. And what added to his surprise was that lady's no personal experience of visiting India. Often he had very enlightening discussion on India's present position. To his utter surprise the foreigners there were supportive to India's 'unity in diversity' concept; only the Brown Sahebs (the Indians influenced by the foreign culture) divided it. He thought to himself 'here I might come across a plethora of such discussions.' But he remained unperturbed.

While lost in his thoughts he was walking towards his college. After a frugal breakfast of bread-butter and hot milk he would leave for his college's library early. Between the beginning of his classes and the opening time of the famous 'Middle Temple Library' there was a couple of hours difference. Since his room was comparatively uncomfortable and library was warm, he would study there only. Even after his classes he would come to the library. He didn't have much money to afford buying costly legal books. Hence he devoted most of the time in library which had all the relevant books on the treatises of law.

The problem that he faced in the library was getting lunch at his free time. One day he happened to meet Mr.

Collestor who ran the canteen there. Vallabh was feeling hungry. He checked his wallet and found only few Cents he could afford to buy something edible. He went to the canteen and asked the gentleman behind the counter.

"Can I get something to eat?"

"Unfortunately, we have the stock exhausted. But you can go to a nearby hotel. It is quite close," replied Mr. Collestor.

"I only want some bread and milk," Vallabh said. "Since I am not familiar with the area, can you help me get bread and milk?"

Mr. Collestor was quite impressed with this simple and straightforward person. He offered to bring the required edibles from that hotel. "But since we are closed, you can't have them here," he said.

"Then please tell me a place where I can have," Vallabh replied giving him some coin for the purchase of the wanted food items.

"Mr. Patel," Collestor said, "I won't accept this money. It is just a trifle."

"No you must, as my helpful dear friend! Because this much help I would be needing every day."

Collestor was touched by this friendly gesture. But he insisted: "That food would be insufficient. You must have something more!"

"I can't have anything else." Patel explained, "First of all I'm totally vegetarian and secondly, if I eat more I'll feel sleepy. Then I can't study and the purpose of coming to the library shall be defeated."

Since that day this frugal lunch was to be arranged everyday. Also, Mr. Collestor would tell him just before six in the evening that it was the time to quit the library.

Seeing Vallabh Bhai Patel's this dedication for studies, not only the people in library and the college, many others also respected him and helped him a lot. So much so, some people started objecting the people showing this much affection to a student from the slave country! Vallabh again thanked his stars for providing this type of help in a foreign land. Eventually he passed two hard exams: the Roman Law and the Bar-at-law in 1st division and returned home in 1913.

***

When Vallabh returned to India, his elder brother Vitthal was doing well as the lawyer. He wanted to participate in the mass uprising against the foreign rule as all the intellectuals were actively jumping into the fire. Vallabh decided to have a categorical talk with Vitthal.

When he reached Vitthal's house in Bombay the later was sitting in his balcony. Seeing his younger brother, Vitthal straightaway broached the topic.

"Vallabh! My conscience is pricking me! I feel guilty of not actively participating in the struggle for national independence. But what checks me is the bitter fact: ensuring the wherewithal for the family! Will it be proper to jump in the fray leaving my roaring practice?"

"Bhai! Had it not been proper so many person would not have done so!"

"But my doing so would create a problem for my family's wherewithal. Then I won't be earning much. One can't ride the two boats simultaneously."

"You join the national uprising and I will see to it that our both families get their needs properly fulfilled."

Vitthal was now reassured; having this problem solved. Vallabh was then based in Ahmedabad which wasn't much far from Bombay where Vitthal's family stayed.

The clientele that Vallabh had established in Godhra also came handy in Ahmedabad where this young bar-at-law had settled following his return from England. His legal practice was doing good. Seeing his clear-headedness and strong logical mind people began to deem him as an authority in legal matters. They wanted him also to join the large section of the intellectual society which was gearing up to take cudgels against the foreign rule. The national awakening in Bengal, based on the reformative and intellectually inspiring principles of Vivekananda and the other moral teachers, dedication of the new leaders like Vipin Chandra Pal, provided much food for thought to the rest of the country. Sage Dayananda's Arya Samaj had also restored the pride among the people of the country's glorious past when India was reckoned as the Teacher of the World (Jagat-Guru). Having lived for three years in England and meeting the intellectuals there, Vallabh had also developed much liking for knowing about India's glory. He distinctly remembered his dialogue with one Professor William. His daughter was planning to visit India when Vallabh was still in England. One evening Prof. William met him in the Middle Temple library and asked him to enlighten his daughter about India.

"Sorry Mr. William! I know nothing about India." Vallabh said flatly.

"What? You don't know about India! Your own country!!"

"Yes! I know only about Bharat."

"Don't play upon words, Mr. Patel. What we call India in English is Bharat in your mother tongue!" William replied.

"Still there is some difference. India is what it is today. Bharat will be and what it had been – the Teacher of the World!"

"But how come your Teacher of the World is under the foreign domination?"

"It is not necessary that a learned man be also politically powerful," Vallabh said.

"I don't catch your point," confessed the baffled William.

"I'll explain. In knowledge, cultural traditions and metaphysical field Bharat is truly pearless in the world. But politically it has become a victim of its power - hungry rulers who sought foreign help to gain authority. But the foreign rulers eventually managed to usurp authority from them. Once they would be removed and Indian leaders realized their past glory, they would soon make India the Teacher of the World again." Vallabh said.

"Okay! But what my daughter should concentrate on reaching India?"

"The roots of Indian culture, its unity in diversity concept, its '*Vasudhaiva Kutumbakam*' idea are some of the topics that will give her a peep into India's perennial reality!"

By that time William's daughter Sophia also joined the discussion.

She asked: "You mean the reality that doesn't change!"

Vallabh: "India's body does change but not its soul which I told you now."

"Won't that be true with all countries – I mean those countries that have existed for long!"

Vallabh: "No… Because your civilization is guided by what we see while India is reckoned by what we feel. The very approach is vastly contradictory. Yours is objective while ours is subjective. Your world is materialistic but ours is spiritualistic. Emotions and relations are more important for the Indians whereas your familid relationship is weaker than us."

Vallabha's arguments were so original and lively that it was often difficult to refute them. He remembered that once he was sitting in his favourite library in London when it was snowing and England was shivering. College friend insisted upon Vallabh having a peg or two of Brandy. "It is extremely cold! Neither you're used to this climate nor you seem to be adequately covered with warm clothes. Brandy shall cover you in a liquid blanket," Henry suggested.

"Thanks for taking care of me. But friend! I shall not even sip a drop of it." Vallabh countered sternly, and added: "My body is sturdy enough to tolerate this cold."

"Your body may catch cold. You'll surely fall ill. And then whole scheduled will be disturbed. It is for your comfort that I insist on you to have a little of Brandy!"

"I won't fall sick. Tell me, should one change his values with the change in climate? Asked Patel and made Henry speechless.

***

"May I come in?" a man knocked at Vallabh's chamber-door in Ahmedabad. Vallabh came back to the present moment from his reverie of the England trip. He found a man seeking his permission to enter his chamber. Vallabh immediately put aside the photographs of his foreign trip and said: "Yes!"

To his surprise he found not one but four men coming in.

"Please be seated. What can I do for you?" Vallabh asked them.

"Sir," one of the gentlemen said: "Although not much time has elapsed to your return from England, I'm sure you must have learnt about the development of the conditions in India."

"Not much, but through the newspapers and my local friends, I have some idea. A new type of the movement has started led by someone called M.K. Gandhi who has also returned from South Africa. Now the Congress Party is quite active under his leadership."

"We all want that you should also join this movement. You can lead us. You have the quality and capacity to lead us in Gujarat. This year a Congress session is likely to take place in Lucknow. We all want you to attend it." The person requested.

"I was already toying with the idea of going there. I am also curious to meet Mr. Gandhi." Vallabh assured them.

That Vallabh had become an important person in Ahmedabad was clear by the series of visitors coming to meet him for various reason. But he was still not very sure of taking an active part in politics. He remembered his commitment to his brother, Vitthal. He had to look after two families. If both the brothers would participate actively in politics, the family's interest will surely suffer.

Next day while he was toying about his possible visit to Lucknow, he found two more visitors at his gate.

Entering in, one of them said apologetically: "Sorry to disturb in this way without any prior appointment. We hope you'll pardon us."

"Oh… it is okay! At the moment I'm not busy," Vallabh said rather graciously.

"Sir," began the apparent leader of the group: "You are a prominent figure of our city."

"I'm glad you think this way. What can I do for you?"

"We invite you to attend our revolutionary programmes that we keep on doing in the city to spread awakening in our country."

"Revolutionary?" Vallabh asked in curiosity.

"Yes Sir, revolutionary! We don't think peaceful efforts will make any impact upon this British Raj. You can't wish them away by your agitations and 'dharanas'. The British have to be pushed out of our country. And if the need be we have to use weapons also," declared the leader rather forcefully. His eyes reflected a firm resolve.

Vallabh thought for a while and then said: "Just a day back some persons came and they suggested my joining the movement started by the Congress under Mr. Gandhi's leadership."

"Sir! We don't find to Gandhi's views reasonable. Do you think that by clearing others latrines and offering your left check if one hits on the right, would help you anyway in uniting the country and cleansing it of the foreigners from our land?"

"Vallabh smiled indulgently and said: "Well, each one can have one's own plans. I know that each one of you have the same destination. Like there could be many ways or faiths to reach the same objective, God! I don't say your way is correct or Mr. Gandhi's is more certain. Of course I wish to see our country freed from the foreign yoke but I don't know whether I can enter the fray. You know my elder brother, Vitthal, has already started actively participating in such endeavours."

"Yes! We have been hearing about him from the Bombay Chronicles."

"So I have to ponder over my line of action, if at all, it is possible," Vallabh said remembering his pledge to his brother about looking after his and Vitthal's families. "Give me some time. But rest assured I am as keen to have our nation arising against the foreign rule."

As the visitors left, Patel was lost in his thoughts. He couldn't have left his and his brother's family in problem for his nationalistic sentiments. He wasn't as much against armed confrontation against the British either. But he also wanted to learn more about this fellow, M.K. Gandhi, whose unique method of protest had forced the South Africa British Rule to toe his line. He wanted to meet Mr. Gandhi personally.

One day Vallabh happened to meet one of his acquaintances who informed him: "You know, Gandhi had built a Satyagraha Ashram on the bank of the river, Sabarmati, near Ahmedabad."

"What is this: a Satyagraha Ashram?" Vallabh asked.

"Ashram is the name for a hermitage. It is a special house in which the dwellers have to follow certain rules. They have to eat very simple vegetarian food and clean their latrines. And in the Ashram all are given equal status.

A few days back Gandhi allowed a family of the very lowly caste to stay there. That has created quite a stir in the entire city."

"What is wrong in that?" Vallabh asked. "I'm sure that must be a human family!"

"All are humans. But will the family members of a low caste sit on the same mat on which the high class family members sit?" that person asked.

"So you have objections to a human being sitting close to you. Well! Mr. Gandhi has his own style to eliminate our social ills."

Although still not convinced about the social transformation that Gandhi was seeking in his own way, Vallabh found Mr. Gandhi to be a different man than all others he met so far. He became quite keen to meet him, and undertook the trip to attend the Congress' Lucknow session of 1916 solely for meeting him.

Remaining busy Gandhi could not give Vallabh much time in Lucknow. Initially Gandhi was also indifferent to him seeing him clad like an Englishman! But later on he met this young bar-at-law from his native place Gujarat and asked: "So… you are a lawyer?"

"Yes Sir! I do my legal practice in Ahmedabad."

"But how come you are drawn to politics?"

"Because this kind of politics is unheard of. It is not only politics but it enshrines in its fold the basic tenets of humanity."

Smiling, Gandhi replied: "Your legal practice will suffer. I, myself, have gone through this phase. In this kind of politics there are no wages. On the contrary, you'll have to put in your resources created by you through other means. It is a kind of 'Begaar' (work without wages) which I also indulge in."

"It is not Begaar when one indulges in it out of one's volition. Working for own land's welfare gives immense satisfaction which is much more that all that money can buy."

Gandhi was impressed with Vallabh more than Vallabh by Gandhi Ji's thinking.

***

In any case Gandhi's influence did encourage him to join active politics. People were willing to bring him into public life. Although Vallabh did have scepticism about enough finances generated to run the two establishments – one in Ahmedabad and other in Bombay – soon he found that his steady clientele would keep that worry at bay.

Gandhi Ji had started his 'self-sanitary' programme in his Ashram which caught people's eye and became a public movement. Coincidently enough, after meeting Gandhi Ji when Vallabh returned to Ahmedabad he was unanimously chosen as a member of Municipal Committee and made the Chairperson of the 'Sanitary Committee'. As his destiny would have it, soon Ahmedabad faced the deadly plague epidemic. Vallabh had some experience of the Godhra plague. In the very first meeting in the capacity as the Sanitary Committee Chairman, his first order was: "Close all schools!"

"And what about the exams?"

"Life is more important than exams. If one survives only then one can appear in the exams."

The epidemic made the Municipality close not only schools but even the courts and Govt. offices as well. Only certain emergency services were maintained with much less attendance. Vallabh was saddled with much work. He was feeling quite restless. All of a sudden he took an unusual decision and informed his colleagues: "Make the citizens leave the city and go to the jungles. Barring the few attending to the patients in the hospitals, let everyone go to jungle. That is the only way we can survive."

It was an unheard decision. But his this decision did manage to lessen the intensity of the horror that epidemic created then. It had its positive effect on the people and now they were quite happy with their new Sanitary Chief of the Municipality.

Although Vallabh Bhai didn't have much participation in the Lucknow Congress Session, he had the knack of seeing through the Gandhi Ji's style of functioning. He soon promulgated a new code of conduct for the Ahmedabad Municipality. It had five basic guidelines:

- The Municipality must play its prominent role in the local self governance.
- This body must fearlessly use its powers for the public welfare.
- No committee should have any nominated members.
- The practice of giving honorific letters to the Govt. officials must be stopped.
- Living quarters must be arranged for the Harijan employees (those from the lowly caste) working in the Municipality.

While preparing this code of conduct Patel was aware that though he entered this urban body through nomination, the people were with him as was revealed by his extraordinary victory in the recent local elections. With this realization, he became all the more dauntless. Now Patel realized that people's support gave so much confidence to the person (him) that he could defy even the tyrannical rule of the British Raj. Even the rich persons of Ahmedabad opened their coffers for him – for they knew that this person was against corruption and would spend even his last paisa for public welfare!

While working this way he learnt about the dictatorial practice of the land revenue officers in the Godhra region. They would yoke the poor farmers in the assigned work without paying them any wages. It was an inhuman practice. Gathering the relevant evidence Patel wrote a long letter to the Commissioner. When the top civil authority of the region failed to respond, Patel had a legal notice sent to him. Since indifference to that notice could have created a legal case, the commissioner had to meet him. Patel met that Englishmen without any fear.

"Please come, Mr. Patel! Have your seat!"

"What made you summon me to your office?"

"I have received your legal notice."

"You must have also received a simple letter from my side a few days back!"

"Oh Yes...! I forgot to reply it."

"You could have forgotten to respond this notice as well. I suspect your Govt. is suffering from selective dementia!"

The commissioner's assistant – the timid Indians – were aghast at Patel's this comment. Fearing a blast from the Englishman, they were amazed when the commissioner quietly said: “You know Mr. Patel things are quite complicated in the peasants’ case.”

“You can remove that complication by tightening a bit your corrupt officers. Else, we have other means also to solve this problem.”

A veiled threat to the Commissioner Saheb! The staff was fearful.

“What do you suggest?” the mellowed commissioner, perturbed by the threat of ‘other means’, tried to settle the issue.

“Stop this Begaar forthwith. Nothing less than this will satisfy us.”

Since Vallabh Bhai had prepared his case with such evidences that even the commissioner could have been chargesheeted. Vallabh Bhai thanked Gandhi Ji in his heart for drawing attention to this practice right under his ken. Of course he fought for the peasants but he got this inspiration from Gandhi Ji.

The Commissioner’s accepting to stop Begaar added yet another feather to Patel’s cap. Although the Municipality was a partially Govt. controlled urban body, the English officers realized that Patel couldn’t be brow-beaten either by racial threats or by legal sophistry. When the Begaar practice was discontinued, Gandhi Ji personally congratulated Patel. He told his secretary: “Patel pursued this case admirably. In his absence things wouldn’t have come to happen so smoothly. He is indeed a very methodical man.”

Gandhi Ji’s main weapon was Satyagraha and his motto was equality of all human beings without any caste and creed consideration. Although Patel in general agreed with these basic principles, he modulated them by his strong logical background. He had seen what Gandhi Ji single handedly achieved in the Champaran Agitation but what revealed Gandhi Ji's true personality was his role in the Kheda Satyagraha.

In Kheda, a part of Gujarat, the farmers were getting increasingly distressed with the mounting cost of the land revenue called 'Lagaan'. When the Administration let loose the suppression tactics, the farmers were incensed and their movement became a big agitation.

Kheda was not far from Vallabh's erstwhile seat of legal practice. He had fought many cases from that area. Taking a direction from Gandhi Ji's fasts in Champaran, Patel also started an agitation in Kheda on a similar pattern. He had the support of his many colleagues like Mohan Lal Desai, Kanti Bhai, Magan Bhai and Anusooiya Ben. However, his colleagues were still skeptical about Gandhian pattern of fight.

In a meeting once Anusooiya Ben warned Vallabha: "You shouldn't forget that the government is run by a foreign ruler!"

"But I am sure the truthful non-violent agitation would awaken the man in the government's dealings. As Gandhi Ji says: 'It is the voice of conscience that should determine our course of action.' And I feel that the government is unjust."

Patel, on Gandhi's instruction had the land revenue collection reports prepared for 400 villages. It was revealed that a nexus between the venal Tehsildars and Deputy Collectors had made all the Patwaris collected more than the revenue that was actually due.

Patel took up this issue to the Government. Gandhi Ji made him the head of the agitation. Patel wrote a long letter to the governor but received no reply. At last a non-violent agitation was launched when the Govt. refused to roll back its decision. Finally their agitation succeeded and the govt. had to withdraw its decision. However, Gandhi was not much satisfied with this achievement. His claim was: "Only a symptom has been neutralized, the disease is still there. We must visit every village and eradicate this oppressive system from its very root."

"We will do so!" Patel said enthusiastically.

Gradually Patel came in closer contact with Gandhi Ji and followed his ideology in true spirit.

***

Around 1919 when the First World War was drawing to its end, things were also changing fast in India. With the novel way suggested by Gandhi Ji and implemented by his latest disciples like Sardar Vallabh Bhai Patel and others, people found a way to exhibit their protest in a peaceful manner. Earlier there were only two available ways: either to suffer oppression or react violently. Now the people know how to protest without showing any violence.

The British Raj was also finding a way to divide and rule. It enacted the most unjust Act infamous as the Rowlatt Act (1919). The expressed objective was better rule of law but the real aim was to create a wedge between its population's two major components: Hindu and Muslim. Such attempts the British Raj had been making right since 1905 when Bengal was divided and also since 1909 when the Morley-Minto Reforms were promulgated. This Act's enactment was most disturbing to all the big leaders of the country including Gandhi Ji and Vallabh Bhai. Lala Lajpat Rai's article in 'Vande Maataram' added fuel to fire by asking Indians not to shake hands with the English men 'whose hands remained stained with our countrymen's blood.'

Vallabh knew that the consequence of this Act's enactment might disturb the Hindu-Muslim unity. While the Hindus believed India to be originally their country, the Muslims claimed that the British had usurped it from their ancestors!"

A country-wide strike was called on 6th April 1919. Gandhi Ji fasted on that day and Vallabh never left him for even a minute during that day. Their closer association brought much respect for each other though there were some differences as well. Gandhi Ji's extra sympathy for Muslims was rather undigestable for Vallabh, though openly he never said it. He also wanted amity between the two major communities of the country but he believed cooperation is a two way passage.

While, one day, talking to his friend, Yagyik, Vallabh clarified his stand: "We must fight on both the fronts."

"Both fronts! What do you mean?" asked Yagyik.

"Against the narrow minded approach of the Muslims and the tyrannical 'divide and rule' policy of the British govt." clarified Vallabh.

"Can we fight against the ruling authority that is trying to divide the two communities?"

"Why not? Don't miss the fact that time and again the people have shown their preference to us."

And Vallabh could reiterate this faith in the people when against the Rowlatt Act he organized protest rallies all over Gujarat. Many agitators were arrested and Ahmedabad's prison began to burst due to large number of prisoners. But Vallabh fought their cases so ingeniously that the Govt. was forced to release them. But the Govt. was hurt. It had to face the defeat from the people. It revenged its hurt by the reckless Jalianwala Massacre which showed its true tyrant face. This tyranical act penetrated deep into Vallabh's heart and then he decided that come what might, he would not rest till these butchers were thrown out of the country.

The Jalianwala Massacre resulted in all the people of the country losing their faith in the so called 'fair-play' of the British government! Even those personages like Ravindra Nath Tagore, who were not directly involved in the political struggle against the foreign rule, also returned their knighthood under protest.

The entire country was inflamed and the people were getting impatient. In that atmosphere , on 4th Sept. 1920 the Congress Session was held under Lala Lajpat Rai's Presidentship in which Gandhi Ji launched his Non-Cooperation Movement. His proposal was passed with a voice vote. Now every awakened citizen of India had one dream: Independence and freedom from the foreign rule. Vallabh Bhai also joined it totally, stopping his legal practice. On 28th Dec. 1921 he organized a huge rally of students and addressed them in his inspired speech: "Come out of your shell with a 'Kafan' on your head! You are the future of our country. Sacrifice your life if the need be to ensure your mother land's honour remaining unscathed." Vallabh become instantly a major figure in the country's struggle and an arch carrier of the flag of Non-Cooperation Movement.

After that speech, Yagyik came to Vallabh and congratulated him: "Vallabh! Your speech is marvelous. But what is the use of invoking the students – for that matter any Indian citizen – to sacrifice their life for country's independence? The ruler is a heartless butcher! Do you think following Gandhi Baba's policy of 'offering your left cheek when your right cheek is slapped' will get you any result? The Govt. won't mind causing yet another massacre. You and your present mentor whom you call Bapu, are casting a pearl before the swine! Expecting sympathy and humane consideration from a stone hearted authority is tentamount to asking for the moon!"

"You could be partially right, friend," Vallabh said after thinking for a while. "But frankly speaking, there is no better way. You can't match the might of the British in an armed confrontation. Of course, there are some hard core nationalists like our daring Subhash Bose, who suggest so, but in the long run you're bound to get in trouble. However, the peaceful movement might succeed as constantly rubbing an ordinary rope on the stone may create a groove. There is no doubt that this is the hard way but a surer way. Hence my belief is in Bapu's way."

Gandhi had clarified the basic steps to agitate against the British. There were five main points:

- Shun all anger and violence.
- Satyagraha even by small institutions and bodies.
- Boycott of the education given by the British Govt.
- Return all the medals and awards given by the Govt. Quit all the Govt. jobs. Wear no foreign-made clothes.
- Boycott all Govt. functions.

And following these points, Gandhi Ji returned all the awards and titles he was conferred with. These happenings encouraged Vallabh to follow suit. He was charged with a new spirit.

Burning the 'Holi' of the hurdles of foreign clothes became a common spectacle. People were resigning from the Govt. posts in a large number. Students keft the Govt. schools and colleges, and joined this National movement. Many such events showed that the Movement was surely gathering momentum.

This Non-cooperation movement's proposal was also tabled in the annual function of Gujarat's political council by no one else but Vallabh Bhai Patel himself which was passed with a thumping majority. The impact of this Movement also affected the family of Vallabh: his children shunned going to their school and he himself ceased to practice as the barrister. He busied himself thoroughly in organizing the agitation in Bardoli on a massive scale. It was to be a totally non-violent agitation. But on 8th Feb. 1922, the agitators became violent in Chauri-Chaura near Gorakhpur and burned down the police station in which 21 constables were burnt alive. Gandhi Ji was so much shocked at the cruelty of the agitators that he suspended the Movement. The entire country was stunned. Patel was also bewildered. He went to Gandhi Ji and asked: "Why this most unexpected decision? Suspending the Movement?"

"It is because our movement was turning violent."

"But one incident in this huge country…!"

"It is not one incident! It shows that people are not following what I want. A little show of violence gives the

Administration an opportunity to use brute force. And it is not according to our ideology."

"But Bapu! Your suspending it would disappoint many."

"And its continuance in this violent way would have made me totally disheartened. You know Patel! It was my moral responsibility to keep this movement non violent. Had I allowed it continue as it is, I'd have gone back on my word! Remember that ours is a moral fight. People believe in what I say. Then I'd have lost my credibility. And the British Raj would have got ample opportunity to use brute force. And then a revolution may have become just an anarchic mutiny."

"But your this decision may give some an opportunity to blame you," said Vallabh, "that you have done it under the pressure from the Govt."

"I don't care what charges are laid on me. For me my conscience is supreme. I can't defy truth. Vallabh! Life is a battle between truth and untruth. If you favour truth the ultimate victory is always be yours. Don't get carried by the transient wave, rather stick to truth."

Patel began to see what Gandhi Ji was driving at. 'Bapu appeared to be giving his Gita discourse,' thought Vallabh, who also realized the strong reason of Gandhi Ji suspending that movement.

However, the suspension of the Movement had wider repercussions. Some sections in the Congress also started saying that Gandhi Ji's main weapon: truth and violence displayed his weakness and not strength. But Patel knew that Gandhi Ji was right. The division in the Congress created yet another party called the 'Swarajya Party'.

These outside events were guiding Patel to a clear way inside his mind. That is why when Gandhi Ji was arrested later on and sent to jail for six years, Patel felt that it would be his moral responsibility to keep the things moving in the way suggested by Bapu. He detected a kind of pessimism clouding the vision of other statwarts like Pt. Nehru and Chittranjan Das. But he decided that no matter what happened he would keep the Movement alive. On 1st Dec. 1922 he organized a big 'Dharana' in the cloth-market of Ahmedabad. His prolonged association with 'Ba' (Kasturba Gandhi, Gandhi Ji's spouse) had made his vision much clearer. He thought as if Gandhi Ji inspiring him through Ba! His one friend, Mohan Bhai Patel did express his doubts. "Vallabh Bhai! I doubt your this Dharana's success."

"I'm doing what I feel just and proper. As the Gita says do your action properly and depend not on the consequence or the result. A devoted action is bound to give you the desired result."

Meanwhile, he was instrumental in establishing the Gujarat Vidyapeeth. He knew that the boycott of the Govt. controlled educational institutions might deprive the people of knowledge. They must have an alternative. Liberal donations from every awakened citizen were collected as much as a million rupees to ease this project's implementation.

While fighting for the national freedom Patel also involved himself in various social, educational, cultural revolutions to create awareness in the people and make them proud of their motherland.

Patel was missing Gandhi Ji very much who was still in jail. He remembered Gandhi Ji's advice: "As they say move the trump when in difficulty, so it is with us, resort to Satyagraha when you feel helpless."

Now he was itching to enter into the arena of direct confrontation. He wanted a Satyagraha must be started from the country's central place, Nagpur. Although the people of Nagpur had no experience of Satyagraha, one such agitation was begun under the leadership of the famous industrialist and Gandhi Ji's arch disciple, Shri Jamanalal Bajaj. The citizens of Nagpur started a huge procession from the posh locality, Civil Lines, of that city.

As the procession proceeded, the police objected: "You can't take procession through this area."

"Why officer? It is a peaceful procession," the agitators said calmly.

"The government doesn't permit it."

"Well! This is our land, we can go anywhere. Why this restriction?"

"Your country is a slave country," the policeman, an Indian, explained.

"You call it a slave country! You're part of us, not a foreigner. Why don't you put off your uniform and join us." Jamanalal Ji said.

"I have children to rear up. I can't risk my job."

"And what about those who are part of this procession. Don't they have their family as well?"

While this discussion was on, suddenly there came an English officer and ordered: "Stop it all, quick!"

"No we won't," refuted a powerful voice.

And the procession continued to move. Jamana Lal Ji was arrested. Patel was behind him. As he was coming to the forefront, his one well-wisher obstructed his way: "No, Vallabh Bhai! Jamana Lal Ji has already been arrested. If you will also get arrested then our this agitation will become leader-less. It may fail."

There, the police-men tore apart their flag. The crowd became violent and in order to avoid violence, the procession was discontinued.

Next day the screaming headlines of the newspapers were: "The flag torn! Jamana Lal Ji arrested! The English officer insulted our flag!"

Even though the procession had been dispersed, its impact was felt all over the country. The despair that engulfed the agitators following Gandhi Ji's arrest was diffused by this Satyagraha. Patel appealed to all the local bodies to join the Satyagraha. Now Nagpur became the hub of the agitations. The bold declaration was made: "We won't stop this Satyagraha! The Union Jack is an English flag, not of India!"

People were charged with Patel's appeal. Hundreds of them reached Nagpur and those who remained away also started their Satyagraha processions in a large number. Vallabh Bhai was delighted to have geared up the movement started by Gandhi Ji. The chant of 'Vande-Mataram' echoed everywhere. The group of volunteers started the 'Prabhat Pheri' (early morning processions) singing aloud: "Jhanda ooncha rahe hamaara!" The atmosphere was electrified.

Even the most optimist agitator never thought that the country could be so charged with patriotism. Kasturba Gandhi also started her 'Female Brigade', for strengthening the agitation.

Nagpur began to look like Prayag during the Kumbha Fair. But here had gathered thousands of 'devotees to the motherland'. The central Province Government was baffled: 'How to stop this Flag Agitation?' It promulgated an order to stop it. But people resisted. At last a via media was found. Patel prepared a letter with his demands clearly specified:

- Hoisting our National Flag is our birthright.
- It is not hoisted to insult any authority.
- It is the basis of our nationalist consciousness.
- Our Satyagraha is for asserting our true rights.

The Govt. also thought it better to accept the same as these conditions had no shade of any rebellion. Eventually the agitators – called Satyagrahis – were released. It was deemed as the partial victory of this Satyagraha. Those who participated actively in this agitation were Shrimati Bhakti Lakshmi Devi from Kheda, alongwith Phool Chanda, Deep Shankar and Shree Krishna Bapu Shah; Mohal Lal Pandey, Shivananda Ji and Balwant Rai Mehta from Saurashtra; Shri Heeralal and Chandu Lal Desai from Bharooch and Shree Dayal Ji, Kalyan Bhai and Champaka Lal Chhiya from Soorat. (Many of these remained close confidants of Vallabha Bhai Patel and earned quite a name, later, in Gujarat politics). Kasturba thanked them all personally. Her active participation in the Satyagraha filled much of the vacuum created by Gandhi Ji's absence.

***

The Nagpur agitation had taken a heavy toll of Vallabh's health. With the result, he fell ill. An ill man naturally remembers his near and dear ones. Vallabh was anxious about his daughter Mani's marriage.

But he was also worried about the dissension creeping in the ranks of the stalwarts of the Congress. Vitthal Bhai, his elder brother had created a forum in Delhi. Pt. Nehru was not happy with Vallabh appearing like Gandhi Ji's main lieutenant. Even the Govt. was unhappy with Vallabh's role in Nagpur. It directed its guns towards this ex-lawyer of Borsad. In Nov. 1923 it held the Borsad Council for protecting the unsocial element in its fold. Before the Council could defend itself, the Govt. penalized it with a hefty fine of Rs. two lakh and forty thousand for its objectionable activities and had the police deputed in its premises.

The council members were upset with these false charges. They had heated discussion: "We must oppose these Govt. fabricated charges," said one, "but how?"

Patel suggested: "I will write a letter challenging the Governor's this move. We shall all move around and publicise our defence against these flimsy charges. I will be personally present in those squads."

Patel's these moves created an atmosphere against the Govt. and the Governor was compelled to make an enquiry against the charges levelled at the Council. It was found that the charges had no base. And the Governor withdrew the penalty order.

That was the time when the Govt. was facing opposition from even the tiny urban bodies all over India. Taking a lesson from Vallabh's moves against the Govt. in the case of Borsad Council, they started their agitations. One such event prominently occurred in Anand where the Govt. had to withdraw its extra-tax order. Now Vallabh Bhai became the really 'Sardar' (headman) for them. Soon this epithet was to become ever prefixed to his name.

***

The events were happening at a fast pace. The Municipality election results were majorly favouring the people's candidates. In Ahmedabad Municipality the Congress got a clear majority. Vallabh Bhai was elected its Chairman. In Allahabad Pt. Nehru became the Chairman of the City Municipality while Dr. Rajindra Prasad was elected Chairman of Patna's Municipality and Dr. Bhagwan Das was elected chairman of Benaras Municipality. The people of India were showing their preference, undaunted by the Govt.'s warth. The stream of national uprising which began with Gandhi Ji's advent on the Ahmedabad's political arena was now flowing all over India, supported by innumerable tiny streams joining from all quarters of the country.

Between 1924 and 1930 the local governing bodies witnessed the increase in the people's participation is local governing bodies. Although the British Govt. in India was quite powerful, it couldn't have neglected the local governing bodies. The govt. ruled by the foreigners had started feeling the minor tremors, heralding an imminent major quake all over the country. Meanwhile Vallabh busied himself in having the misunderstandings removed amongst the top leaders of the Congress.

But soon a major flood began to devastate the city of Ahmedabad. He started to work in the flood-relief camps. They needed huge funds. Magan Bhai Desai suggested: "We must form a big organization on temporary basis under which we collect food, clothes, medicines for the flood victims."

Patel suggested: "Also a big team of the doctors."

Magan Bhai said: "I think we must inform Vitthal Bhai to arrange for some help." Vitthal was then the speaker of the Central Assembly. His efforts not only made the Govt. accept their demand and release one crore rupees for the Flood Relief Centre but only allowed Vitthal to visit Nadiad personally.

While tackling this major problem in Gujarat, Vallabh Bhai had his name recognized all over the country. This sun's rays were now illuminating upto the other end of the horizon. His efforts in the flood relief was recognized even by the local administration. The Ahmedabad collector publicly honoured Vallabh Bhai. Not only that, the Chairperson of the East India Cotton Association, Sir Purushottam Das, sent a huge amount to Patel for the relief of the flood victims. Patel loved helping people. He was emerging as the Messiah of the distressed persons.

Feeling somewhat relieved Patel now began to sort out some family problems. He wanted his daughter Mani Bhen to get married. He and his mother tried to impress upon Mani to get ready for marriage. But despite their efforts she remained adamant and refused to heed to their advice. "Perhaps she has other designs for her future. Let it be what God desires," thought Vallabh.

However, there emerged yet another problem from Bardoli which had special soft corner for Vallabh due to his earlier association. It was a well irrigated region as there were three rivers surrounding it. It was generally quite green and quite fertile. The region covered around 400 square miles. But a part of this region was not so fertile wherein the farmers had to labour a lot.

Its western region was quite developed which was spotted by the government. It straightaway raised the revenue rate by 30 percent. It also developed as a politically conscious region due to its proximity to Bombay as well as direct connection with Baroda state which was quite advanced in its own right.

This raise in the revenue collection rate was objected by many big leaders in including Rai Bahadur Bheema Bhai Nayak and Dadu Bhai Desai who also raised this issue in Bombay's State Assembly. But nothing came of it. Then they met Patel. He could feel the pain suffered by the local farmers since he was also a farmer's son who had suffered such agony himself. With the result on 2nd March 1928 he left for touring the region of Bardoli himself.

***

Patel reached Bardoli around evening when the dust by the movement of the bullocks with their masters was rising high. The farmers were rather tired but cheerful seeing their favoured leader coming to Bardoli. Patel was very much concerned about them. He advised the farmers: "Don't feel disheartened. We will do something. I will discuss this matter with Bapu also. But remember: we have to do Satyagraha. It may call for patience and much tolerance. Remember that we had scored our point with the government in Kheda and Borsad with this strategy. But you all shouldn't fear. This is your land and you have every right to earn your bread from it. This land has not been imported by the foreign Govt. from England. Why should you fear?"

Patel's advice influenced the farmers and they ceased to give the land-tax to the Govt. Also, Patel wrote a long letter to the Governor saying: "This part of the land shouldn't have the tax-rate enhanced at all. The farmers are quite hard-pressed to give the tax at the previous rate itself. I request you to institute an enquiry committee which should assess the correct land rate tax for this region."

But the Govt. (Governor) didn't respond. The farmers asked:

"What should we do now, Sardar?"

"We must build our strength by asking all the farmers to join in this protest movement. We must visit as many villages as possible. And be wary of the Govt.'s old policy of 'divide and rule'. We must take an oath to remain united come what may."

Sardar Patel made them ready to face any eventuality. He also created 14 centres in Bardoli region, covering separate blocks of village and under the leadership of his trusted fellow members. It was Sardar's far-sighted vision that made Bardoli Movement a touchstone of impressing upon the Govt. of people's strength. He made people decide that should the Govt. go for auctioning any one's land, no one should come forward. Not only that "provide no service or facility to the visiting Govt. officials in this region."

The Govt. came up with its cunning declaration containing the following conditions:

- The tax-levy order should not be reduced if it exceeded 25% or more.
- That enhanced tax should be immediately paid.
- Where there is more than 50% that should be deemed reduced to 25%.

The people saw through this confusing game. They refused to fall in the Govt.'s trap. It sent its various officials with a variety of tricks but Sardar's strategy made their efforts futile. They also resorted to selling off people's landed properly but got no buyers. This kind of unity among the farmers was rather unprecedented. Even some of the English Newspapers came up with the editorials: "Bardoli has almost the self-rule now!"

The Govt. was baffled. It felt totally isolated as even the womenfolk came up to support their male counterparts. They would move out in their group chanting slogan in Sardar's honour and singing songs highlighting this Satyagraha. Between Feb. 1928 and June 1928 Bardoli Satyagraha emerged as the most potent movement ever started by the people. Gandhi Ji sent his blessings through Seth Jamnalal Bajaj. Gandhi Ji himself rendered his full moral support to Bardoli Satyagraha by openly declaring: "Helping Bardoli Movement is equal to helping yourself!"

Gandhi Ji's this open declaration made this Satyagraha almost a national movement. Those who were indifferent to it joined it with double enthusiasm. Bardoli Satyagraha emerged as the laurel for Sardar Patel, his most prominent achievement prior to India's independence. He became the part of the folk-lore and the hero of the folk songs. At places his name became a beacon attracting even the Indians serving the British Raj. Bombay newspapers were full of their detailed coverage. A report published in the Times of India summed up this Bardoli Movement's impact in the following words:

"Bombay Administration also runs upto Bardoli where Mr. Gandhi has started the experimentation with his kind of Bolshevism and it is succeeding very well. The Govt. machinery is totally ineffective there as Sardar Patel's writ runs there, the 'Lenin' of the region."

***

Bardoli Movement presented a great dilemma before Sardar Patel's elder brother, Vitthal Bhai who was the Speaker with Central Assembly. He was in a great fix: 'What should to do? Continue to work as the Speaker of the Central Assembly or should resign and join this Satyagraha with my brother.' On one hand he had to ensure the financial security of his family but on the other his voice of conscience which forced him to go to Bardoli and stand with his dedicated brother, Vallabh. At last, he decided to seek Gandhi Ji's opinion. He wrote: "Under the present circumstances neither I can sit quietly nor could be indifferent toward Bardoli Movement. As for the financial assistance you referred about, sending one thousand rupees with this letter. Regrettably, despite my sympathies with the Bardoli farmers, I can't start any solid constructive work for them. Against the Govt.'s most damaging policy there is no option but to surrender and I find my hands tied. However, I still hope that the Bardoli Movement will continue and I shall continue to contribute some amount. I have got this post due to their support. I also want to support this movement. I promise to do my utmost effort for this. If I learn that apart from the financial help, the Satyagrahis need something else, I assure you that I will not move back!"

In fact not only the known and reputed but also many obscure and unknown persons kept on sending financial help for this Bardoli Satyagraha. Even the Govt. was amazed at the Satyagrahi's financial help. It could not ascertain as to what was their source of income. "How they could organize so many protests, demonstrations, Kisan Sabhas and Prabhat Pheri's when the officials had deprived them of their source of income?" The Govt. got confused.

At last, a moment came when the Govt. invited Vallabh Bhai for peace-negotiations. When he received the Governor's letter, Vallabh was happy no doubt – at last the struggle coming to an end, and the farmers would now lead their normal life. But he was in no mood to rush to the Governor's home immediately. He thought it better to list out his conditions for the negotiations. These were no less than a public order that "if you accept them, we will be willing to negotiate peace."

His main conditions were:

- Return the goods and landed property of the farmers and the peasants forcibly auctioned by the Govt. officials.
- All the dismissed Patwaris should be restored back to their erstwhile services without any loss in their seniority.
- Those who have resigned should be absorbed back into their original position without any positional and financial loss.

There were however some selfish money-lenders who had purchased the farmer's land in auction out of their greed and also to please the Govt. officials. They were unwilling to return the land without getting their money. The matter reached upto Sardar's level and he enquired from the money lenders. They said: "Sir! We will return their land provided we get back our money."

Sardar said: "The money will be returned by the Govt. department where it was deposited in the first place."

They said: "If you could help us, we have no objection to return their lands."

Many such problems were emerging in the village. Patel had to intervene in almost every case. But Patel's suggestion was accepted by all and the storm appeared to be subsiding.

So far there were protests, demonstrations and now people had meetings to honour their leaders and shower encomiums on them. By this time Patel had become a 'Mythical God' almost for the Satyagrahis.

An old lady, deeming Sardar Patel to be her darling son, composed a in the rustic Gujarati which became instantly popular.

"Naanya thaare paalanei, naache re banmor
'Gutur gu' kar geet sunaave
Kalijiche ri kor
'Choon-choon' chidakali chuggey – chugaave
Halrare bhar jor
Naanya thaare paalanei, naache re banmor!
Saaras kare kilola thare, paalniye ri chhor
Teetar phiregee olyoon dolyoon
Chide-chide re jor
Naanya thaare paalanei, naache re banmor!
Koyal geet Badhaave gave, hale resham dor
Tihoonka tihorhi aave – jaave, baith machave shor
Haryo suvaro thare paalnei, heende resham dor

Polyan thaaro paalano, hivade bhare hilor

Naanya thaare paalanei, naache re banmor!

Many such songs were created to wish immortality to their dotted son – Sardar Patel. Many conferences were held to felicitate Sardar for his unprecedented leadership qualities. Often in Gujarat he was respected as Arjun while Gandhi Ji as Yogeshwar Krishna. A popular poet of that period, Narsimha Rao wrote: (using a famous sloka of the Gita):

"Yatra Jogeshwaro Gandhi,
Vallabhashcha Dhanurdharah!

Tatra Shree Vijayo Bhooti Dhrurva Neetir Matirmam!"

(Victory is assured where valiants like Yogeshwar Gandhi and the great archer Vallabh are present.)

And when the great performer works in tandem with truth, nobody can stop his victory campaign.

***

As the hero of the Bardoli Satyagraha, Vallabh received many bouquets from a variety of fields. He was emerging as a true leader of masses. But his spectacular rise in the political field emerged as an anathema to many other persons including some of the Congress's old stalwarts. Vallabh was aware of these inside developments but he was more worried about the nasty moves that he expected the Govt. to make. He listed them inside his mind. His potential worry causing were three moves:

- Inside bickering within the Congress due to his own spectacular rise.
- The Govt.'s possible move to create a wider rift between the Hindus and the Muslims.

- The conspiracy by some Govt. instigated vested powers to alienates lower strata of the Hindu society by misconstruing history.

While he was busy mentally brooding over his strategy to counter these sinister tendencies, he was baffled one day when his daughter, Mani's putting forth a startling proposal.

"Which way are we moving towards, Bapu,?" she asked Vallabh whom she lovingly called Bapu (Gujarati equivalent of 'father').

"Towards Swarajya," replied Vallabh.

"Swarajya meaning…?" she asked.

"Meaning our own rule… redemption from the foreign domination!"

"How do you propose to achieve it.? By making people revolt against the British… Isn't it? But Bapu… that way you can get only half freedom… Because unless the Indian women are made educated and self-dependent, you can't have total freedom."

"Oh yes!" Agreed the baffled father. He didn't know that his daughter had grown up… her thinking process had become quite mature!

While Vallabh Bhai was still in thoughts, Mani continued: "And this way I propose to help you all by starting a women awakening campaign. I have already talked about it with Gandhi Ji and he gave me the green signal. I'll remain with you and shall work in this field. After all we females have also to do our duty in the struggle for independence… I hope you'll agree with me."

"Sure…sure, my child! But remember we are Gandhi Ji's soldiers who fight with only two essential weapons: Truth and Non-violence."

"That I know. I have participated in Ba's (Kasturba's) women squads. I hope you have no inhibition about my such participation in your struggle for independence."

"Not at all, dear! You have my full support." Said Vallabh.

Now he realized what was cooking in his daughter's mind and why did she refuse to marry when he and his mother asked her to marry. Seeing her face aglow with new resolve he found his worry on this account completely dissolved in the light radiating from her face!

But Vallabh couldn't say to his mother about what decision his daughter had taken with his support! He knew that his mother will violently oppose it. He decided to postpone this session with his mother as the Calcutta Session of the Congress was round the corner. His national duty again took precedence over his familial duty.

***

In the end of Dec. 1928 the Calcutta Session took place. It had three important developments: first Motilal Nehru was chosen the President, second the Bardoli hero (Patel) received the special honour for his spectacular victory against the Govt. and the third and the most important was the demand of the Indian dominion status. This Session threw special lime-light on the Nehru family.

Meanwhile, taking an inspiration from Bardoli, in Madras region Rajgopalachari spread the similar agitation defying the Govt.'s oppressive rule. Patel's address given on that sultry day in the Marina Beach surged forth a new wave of peaceful rebellion among the people of South India.

When Patel returned to Ahmedabad he received a special call from Gandhi Ji through Gandhi Ji's secretary Mahadeva Desai.

By this time Vallabh had become a confidant of Bapu. Apart from the similarity of their thinking pattern, they had the advantage of the common mother tongue. Vallabh found Gardhi Ji in quite a sombre mood.

"The Viceroy has refused to toe our line. They are unwilling to discuss even the dominion status to us. If we don't oppose the Govt. we may lose the support of the people. What should we do to remind the British Raj about our unified stand?"

While Patel was thinking, suddenly Gandhi Ji had an idea,

"Let us break the Salt-law. Manufacturing salt is our basic right."

Patel couldn't catch his line of thinking,

"Breaking salt laws? What we'd gain from it?" he asked.

"Look Vallabh! Following the boycott of the Simon Commission, the country is getting inflamed with the Govt. repressive measures. Any time the people can resort to violence. They need to be kept in check. Mere appeal to them won't do the needful. We must 'Do' something to ensure catharsis of their sentiments against the Govt. We must show our peaceful defiance to the Govt.'s rule. In that way, breaking salt is very useful. Salt is everyone's essential item. It is our basic necessity. Its price affects everyone's budget. We can say that any tax on the salt infringes upon our basic right. We shall break the salt laws."

Patel was amazed at Bapu's (Gandhi Ji's) power of assessing the countrymen's mood and psyche. He also found it to be very ingenious idea. 'There is no doubt that these laws affect even the poorest of the poor. Salt is everybody's basic need,' Vallabh was thinking. He was still amazed at this brilliant idea. Much later, once Gandhi Ji confided his taking this idea from Lord Krishna's activities. The Bhagwat clearly says that when the tyrannical ruler of Mathura, Kansa, promulgated the order that entire milk and its products would first be brought to his palace and after the royal cut, it could be taken back by the Gwalas (cow-men) who were their basic producers. Lord Krishna (or the child-Krishna at that time) asked the common Vraj-Vasis (dwellers of the Vraj region) to defy this order of Kansa as the producer of the product had his first right on it. That was why he asked them not to take milk, whey, butter etc. to Mathura at all and those Gopis who did so had their pitchers full of the products broken by Krishna and his friends. Gandhi Ji's argument was similar. 'Making salt is our birth right. Why should we pay tax on it?"

Everybody liked the idea. But Patel (Vallabh) said: "Bapu! It has to be a controlled agitation. Else it could turn violent in a flicker of an eye-lid."

"Yes! That we have to guard against. I shall myself lead this movement."

"We must choose only those who truly believe in non-violence," suggested Patel.

And soon Gandhi Ji declared that he was against Salt-laws and inspired people to break them after he had shown the way. He asked Patel and his other trusted lieutenants to spread this awareness in the people and ensure no violence emerged from this agitation.

Gandhi Ji selected a place called Dandi (in Gujarat), not far from the coastal area where salt was manufactured.

Then according to the charted programme, on 6th April 1930, Gandhi Ji started his Civil Disobedience Movement with his historic march to Dandi to break the Salt Laws. The movement, aiming at strikes, boycott of British goods and a general attitude of disobedience towards the ruling authority, spread to all parts of the country. This gave rise in the North West Frontier Province (Kabul etc.) the Red Shirt Movement under the leadership Khan Abdul Ghaffar Khan (who later came to be known as Frontier Gandhi). More than 60,000 people were arrested and jailed. A reign of terror and repression was let loose by the Govt. to arrest the tempo of the movement.

Vallabh Bhai had done much publicity to make this movement a grand success. He was arrested on 7th March itself before he could participate in the Dandi March and before he could address a large rally. The Govt. framed a tiny case and arrested him for four months, Sardar's arrest made the people more committed to do what was left undone by their leader.

They took a resolve publicly: "We shall follow the path shown by our revered leader, Sardar Vallabh Bhai Patel and shall continue doing so till we become independent. Unless we remove this foreign rule, we shall neither take rest nor shall this Govt. heave a sigh of relief."

This pledge taken by the people of Ahmedabad resounded through the entire length and breadth of the country.

There, Sardar Patel, passing time in the prison was reminded of a talk he had following the Calcutta Session.

"You know Vallabh," Gandhi Ji said: "Why I declined to become the President of the Congress?"

"Bapu," Vallabh said: "I never doubt your decisions. I am sure they are ever based on a sound judgement."

"In fact, I want the youth of the country should come forward. We have our time limited in the world. I'm already past 60."

"I'm also beyond 50," Patel said.

"That is why I think Jawahar Lal should be a better candidate. He is around 40. He has the backing of three provinces."

"All right. He is a fine choice."

"I want," Gandhi Ji said, "this time our movement must deprive the Govt. of its beauty-sleep. But it has to be totally non-violent. We seek not only the political independence. We must deserve it. We are dispirited at many levels."

"But Bapu," Patel opined: "We do unite at the time of Satyagraha."

"But only during that phase. We must learn to remain ever united. If we learn this, we shall remain united even after independence. Else we may lose it again."

***

Now the political events were happening in a very fast pace. In 1930, in the Congress Session held in Lahore, on the banks of river Ravi, Jawahar Lal Nehru was unanimously chosen as the President, and the Congress under his leadership declared: "We want total freedom. We won't accept any compromise on it." The Tricolour was unfurled and with it was declared that on 26th Jan. the call for 'Poorna Swarajya' would also be given.

Patel was still in prison when these events took place. He felt that the light of freedom was round the corner and he was seeing the end of the dark tunnel. He felt as though Gandhi Ji was before him and explaining the meaning of the Poorna Swarajya. "Poorna Swarajya should make you feel freedom in body and spirit. In that you shouldn't ask as to what the country can give to you… instead you should give all that you can to the country. That is Swarajya which gives you the feeling of unity, which develops mutual confidence and faith in the countrymen."

Suddenly he was brought to his grim present. He was still in the prison and the warder was knocking at his cell gate to deliver the tray of food. But Vallabh didn't feel any appetite. He was seeing his long past, a tiny fraction of the present and an infinite future. Vallabh was traversing in a fleeting way in each of them. Now he felt he was in Borsad, now in Godhra… then in England… and suddenly in the present prison cell getting the glimpse of the shining future. At that time his food was his reflective mood. He began to move around in that tiny cell. He felt as if someone is showering flowers on the roof of his cell!

When Gandhi Ji was arrested following the Dandi March, Motilal Nehru took the reigns of guidance in his hands to keep the chariot of the Congress Party moving. Vallabh was quite lonely and his memories gave him the sole company. He recalled the moment when he first met Gandhi Ji:

He was going to Sabarmati Prison from Borsad.

"Will I be allowed to stay in Sabarmati for sometime?"

"Do you want to meet Gandhi Ji?"

"That is precisely the purpose I am here for."

He was allowed to go in. He was before a person of a nondescript personality but his face had a kind of glow. His eyes were saying. "So we can work together, Vallabh."

***

During that period, prison had become the favourite meeting point for the Satyagrahis. Many of the old generation came in contact with those of the new generation. Patel also met many of his old friends and also befriended some of the new ones. Hari Prasad Desai, Gokuldas Talaati, Ramdas Gandhi were some of them. From them he learnt about the Dandi trip of Gandhi Ji. In prison, the jailer was quite impressed with Patel and he sought to give him special food. But Vallabh refused. He said: "Give me whatever is given to the common prisoner." He wanted to use meal time to exchange notes with the new and old generation and learn from the common people as to what impact they felt of Gandhi Ji's movement. He passed his time in assessing his role in the Gandhi Ji's movement and chart his future course of action accordingly.

At last his day of release from the prison dawned. On 26th June 1930 he was released.

Meanwhile, following Gandhi Ji's arrest, Motilal Nehru was guiding the movement. He also realized the foul intention of the government concocting reasons to arrest all big leaders. Motilal Ji was anticipating his arrest any time. So he made Patel the interim President of the Congress, saying: "this chair shouldn't remain vacant!"

People were also becoming restless. Once Patel gave such a fiery speech that the entire crowd thundered with slogans "Bharat Mata Ki Jai… Vande Mataram!" etc.

The CID officer deputized by the Governor to assess the public mood was quite nervous. He gave his report to the Governor. He was in a fix. While the head of the Administration wanted a stern action on the Satyagrahis, the public mood indicated a bitter backlash causing major law and order problem. The Governor asked his secretary: "What do you suggest? Should we pounce upon them to pulverize their morale?"

"I wouldn't advise that Sir! Things may go out of hands once we show force."

"Shouldn't we declare the Congress to be an illegal organization?"

"What?"

"Yes… I mean it," said the Governor. He was desperate.

And the Governor declared the Congress to be an illegal organization and imposed a ban on it!

But this added fuel to the fire already burning in the people's heart. On 13th July 1930 Patel opposed this banning ordinance and inspired the people. The situation had become quite volatile. The speech of the Viceroy, Lord Irwin, in the Central Assembly further stoked the fire when he declared that that Govt. would crush this Disobedience Movement. Undaunted, Sardar also gave another speech in which he fully supported Nehru's call for 'Poorna Swarajya' (Total Self-Rule).

The Govt. sent the police to seal many Congress offices. Patel was forcefully opposing this Govt.'s oppression through his speeches. Meanwhile, came Tilak's 75th birthday which was celebrated with great enthusiasm in Bombay despite the Govt.'s unwillingness. In the procession there were great stalwarts like Lala Lajpatrai, Madan Mohan Malviya and Sardar Patel. This huge procession was stopped by the police squads. But the agitators remained unmoved and staged a Dharana on the road itself. Their firm resolve was further tested by a heavy rainfall. But no one moved away. They continued to remain squatted on the road whole night. The policemen were amazed for even the women remained undaunted by the natural and the Govt. created disturbances.

A huge number of the police parties surrounded the procession from every side. Sardar Patel was taken as prisoner. In fact whoever protested was arrested. The prisons overflew with the arrested agitators. At that time no prison of the country was devoid of the freedom fighters. Such was the influence of Gandhi Ji that every Indian was suspected to be a Congress-member and every house was deemed a Congress office. Reflecting upon the existing situation once Sardar Patel himself said: "The Congress has turned into a synonym for the struggle for independence!"

The tyrant British Rule was at its wit's end. In utter desperation to control the situation its Administrators had become totally inhuman. The tortures that the people were subjected to, were unimaginable and extremely painful.

Sardar Patel was imprisoned for three months. The police squads even raided his house in his absence to search for any objectional evidence. It was around the noon time when they seized the house. Sardar's mother was busy preparing her lunch. She was above 80 years old at that time. The police resorted to such lowly acts like throwing the prepared food on the ground and also put dirt into it to make it totally unedible. Enraged 'Ladba' (Sardar's eighty plus mother) pushed away the policeman who did so. He fell down quite away. The Iron-man's mother had much strength still left in her old bones: "Be off… you fool!"

"Keep quiet you oldie!" retorted the policeman.

"No I won't. It is time your Govt. stopped this nonsense! It will have to keep quiet when my lion-hearted son roars!"

Taken aback at that old woman's audacity, the police party retreated, completing the bare formalities of the raid!

After sometime Sardar Patel was released. But the Govt. banned his speeches. But can a lion keep quiet when the dogs bark? Sardar kept on addressing people whenever he could. With the result the Govt. had him arrested for nine months. This time he was imprisoned in the Yervada jail.

***

In the political firmament of India it appeared as if the day of reckoning was not far off. The country was becoming restive increasingly. Despite diverse faiths, religions and communities, the people of India had one solitary aim: "oust the foreign rule; send these red-faced monkeys back to the land they belong! Enough is enough!" Although the movement was somewhat sluggish, the fire that spread to all the corners had started giving flames. The British Government realized that despite its imprisoning all the big leaders of the Congress or of this mass movement, the people were not downcast. They had the rebellion writ large on their face. Now the Govt. understood that they could no more be taken for granted.

Lord Irwin was in the seat of the Viceroy. He was sending repeated messages to England, detailing the 'unpleasant situation' developing in India. The British had this sad realization that their authority was weakening in India. They had to do something about it.

At last under the chairmanship of the British Prime Minister, Ramsay Macdonald, a round table conference was summoned. Although physically the Congress was not represented in it, the whole conference had the shadow of this party influencing all the participants. The declaration from the British Prime Minister was needed to make India receive a Dominion status.

The indications were clear that Mighty British Crown was about to face its first major threat from the slave Indians. With its varied experience as the colonial ruler, the British Crown knew that India could no more be neglected in its present state of turmoil. Hence the Crown granted the Dominion Status to India, and Gandhi, Patel and others were released from the prison, with this 'Gandhi – Irwin Pact', coming into being. This was the first pact with the British Govt. which did open a little passage for India's freedom. But much was still needed to be done.

Nevertheless the 'Gandhi – Irwin Pact' ensured the release of all the political prisoners and according to the agreement reached, the Civil Disobedience Movement was also withdrawn.

The Congress' Karachi Session took place in 1931 in which apart from accepting the Gandhi-Irwin Pact it was also decided that Gandhi Ji would personally represent the Congress in the imminent Second Round Table Conference. It was held in England on 15th Sept with Gandhi Ji representing the Congress, but despite all efforts it failed. The bone of contention was the Hindu-Muslim mutual agreement. Many thought it was done deliberately at the instructions of the Crown. Because the British had realized that the only way to weaken the public-power in this country was to create and maintain a wedge between the Hindus and the Muslims. The Muslims, led by their narrow minded leaders like Jinnah, had their dreams revived of holding their authority over the large part – if not full Hindustan– as they had before the arrival of the 'East India Company'.

History doesn't record any document proving Gandhi Ji's smelling this rat in the British mind but Patel had smell the foul game, though he never expressed openly.

Vallabh had such regard for Gandhi Ji – whom he called Bapu and deemed him to be a saint – that he could never openly say anything that might hurt his Bapu's feelings. But he new what was cooking in the Govt.'s mind. The British Raj, already hurt with the massive failure of the Second Round Table Conference was awaiting its opportunity to strike. It found a clue in enquiry of the Bardoli Episode in which the Govt. had played a dirty role.

The Govt. instituted an enquiry commission to reveal the iniquities the farmers were subjected to, in Bardoli. While Mr. Garden represented the Govt., Bhoola Bhai Desai respresented the agitators. On Patel's suggestion Mr. Desai insisted on including all the orders that the Govt. passed during the period this episode continued, which Mr. Garden refused to agree. At last the enquiry ended without drawing any final conclusion.

***

When Gandhi Ji returned from London, Willingdon became the new Viceroy of India. But Willingdon was in a belligerent move. He refused to meet even Gandhi and instead of trying to find a peaceful way to settle the disputes with the Congrss, he declared this party as illegal or even unlawful political organization. The Govt. started its cycles of tyranny and oppression; it was growing increasingly aggressive. Willingdon particularly chosen for his ruthless ways of working. The Crown was now willing to fight a categorical battle.

The Govt. continued to fan the communal sentiment to make Jinnah come as an adversary of Gandhi. In order to deepen the chasm between the Hindus and Muslims it wanted clearly demarcated constituencies for the Hindus and Muslims.

This suggestion was unacceptable to the Congress led by Gandhi Ji. "How could I have accepted this divisive arrangement?" Gandhi Ji confided in Patel. Patel also wanted to warn him about the dirty game the Govt. was planning using Jinnah, as a tool. He wanted Gandhi Ji to use his influence over the section of the nationalist Muslims but Bapu might say: "Vallabh! get over these petty feelings."

Soon the resentment of the people of United Provinces (as U.P. was known then) spread to the entire country and demonstrations began. Even the Congress president then, Vallabh Bhai was also arrested. But he had left a good team of the able leaders who kept the agitation alive.

As the coincidence would have it; this time Gandhi Ji and Vallabh Bhai were put in the same prison. Gandhi Ji apprehended that the Govt.'s this divisive game might also alienate the Harijans (lowly class) from the Hindu fold. He would frequently talk about the Harijan leaders and try to convince them to remain in the Hindu fold. Since the Govt. was working on these divisive policy, Gandhi Ji and Patel were quite alert. One day they heard that the Govt. was creating the separate representative of the Harijans. He was worried seeing Gandhi Ji very much disturbed. They talked about the issue and finally Gandhi Ji sent a telegramme to the British PM. Fortunately his view was accepted. Meanwhile Gandhi Ji also had a detailed meeting with Mr. B.R. Ambedkar, the most recognized leader of the lowly castes – Harijans. However the Harijan leaders were not convinced. Discerning their adamance Gandhi Ji declared his 'Anshan' (fast) to prevent alienation of the Harijans. Although initially Ambedkar had his reservations about Gandhi Ji's stand on the Harijan, yet in the larger interest of the national unity, Ambedkar accepted Gandhi Ji's point. The Harijans continued to be recognized as honoured citizens of India and Ambedkar began to be accepted as one of the top leaders of India.

***

While Sardar Patel was in jail, he met a few revolutionaries also. He had a soft corner for them: "these young persons, hardly beyond 20 or 25, burning with the desire of eliminating the British from India and liberating their 'Bharat Ma'. He remembered when before the Karachi session of the Congress, they received the most heart-rendering news of hanging of Bhagat Singh and his two companion. He had a mild tiff with many of his associates. He said: "The path of these revolutionaries may be violent but their destination is as pure as Ganga. Just see at what age have they sacrificed their life? What did they expect in return? Nothing? The coming generation might not even know about their sacrifice." And despite some opposition, as the Congress President he issued a scathing condemnation of the British Raj's policies to deal with these revolutionaries. He remembered how the mean Govt. had sown the seed of communal disharmony between the Hindus and the Muslims which resulted in the gory riots, in particularly north India, in which a fearless journalist, Ganesh Shankar Vidyarthi had lost his life in Kanpur. Patel had great respect for Bhagat Singh, Chandra Shekhar Azad and his cohorts. Once he had an argument with even Gandhi Ji, saying "I also abhor violence but we must see under what circumstances that violent act is committed. Fighting for one's motherland if one indulges in violence it is always better than the non-violence displayed even when one's mother's honour is in danger." But following Bhagat Singh and his companions hanging and the Governments stealthily getting the last rites performed left a deep scar in Patel's heart. He was now convinced that this morally deprived Govt. could stoop to any level to achieve its vile objectives. His hatred for the British Raj was again revived when, he heard that despite the Round Table Conference's agreement, the Govt. was recklessly arresting all the top leaders of the country, going back on its words.

But the Govt. was adamant. Between 31st March & 1st April 1931 many more leaders were arrested. When the Congress Session was taking place under the chairperson Smt. Nalini Sengupta, more than 240 persons were arrested in a single day.

That night Sardar couldn't sleep. He could realize the agony the Gandhi Ji could have been going through. He was sorry that he couldn't go near his Guru to provide him some solace, nor he could go out to help his countrymen at all. He would walk a bit in his small cell and after sometime would stretch out on his cot. He was much perturbed. Even his personal life was giving him no relief. Following the Civil Disobedience Movement, his elder brother, Vitthal Bhai has resigned from the post of the speaker of the Central Assembly. Owing to his active participation in the movement, he was also arrested. While in jail Vitthal became seriously ill. On compassionate grounds, he was released and sent to Europe for his treatment.

It was a period of suddenly caused almost vacuum in the ranks of the Congress. While most of the leaders were in the prison, those out of it had fallen ill. Even Subhash Chandra Bose was ill so seriously that he had to go Europe for the treatment.

And then a series of tragedies happened in the life of Patel. His elder brother expired, followed by his mother's death. And not much time elapsed when Dayabhai's (his son's) wife also expired. Sardar Patel, the Iron-Man, was finding these tragedies quite unbearable. While his mother's cremation was done by his another brother and that of his daughter-in-law's by Dahya Bhai, Sardar wanted to attend his brother Vitthal's cremation. He requested the jail authorities to release him on parole. But the heartless British Raj put forth some disrespectful conditions for his release. He was in a great fix. He consulted Mahadeva Bhai who was there:

"What should I do? Write a letter to Bapu and seek his opinion?"

"Remember," Mahadeva said, "that the Govt. would, this way, be obliging you and your morale will be shaken. I think this would also be Bapu's advice."

"Then I'd not go to attend Vitthal's cremation," Sardar said in his typical style.

"But you'll feel sorry, Vallabh," Mahadeva said.

"When I jumped into this fire, such situations are not unexpected. I have to bear them for my commitment to my country." Then heaving a long sigh: "Everyone is not so fortunate as Subhash (Chandra Bose) is who could remain for long with his brother's body!"

And bearing a load of agony in his heart Sardar refused to get released on parole under so demeaning conditions. He said openly: "I cannot compromise on Satyagraha for the sake of my personal tragedy."

And so he couldn't attend his most beloved brother's cremation. Day in and day out he kept remembering his brother who was so dear to him. "Bharat Ma needs such sacrifice from her every committed son."

Not only that he didn't go even to see his typhoid stricken only son, later on, since the Govt. again put forth such insulting conditions again for his release on parole. He had developed infinite capacity to bear personal tragedies and yet move on his path undeterred. He was truly an Iron Man!

But only few days later, his nose had some big problem and the operation was unavoidable. At last for getting his nose operated he was released. Nehru and Badshah Khan were still in the prison. The Govt. couldn't dare releasing such big leaders in one go. Nevertheless the spark that the

Congress leaders had created in the countrymen's hearts for freedom was gradually acquiring flames. Indications of the mass uprising had begun to appear in the various parts of the country.

***

The British Raj could realize that its count down for exit from India had begun. 'The Sun that never sets' had become a victim of the shadows of the imminent eclipse.

The European firmament had been covered by the war planes. The World War was spreading and Japan was quickly threatening with its forces advancing towards South East. The Indian leaders were in a fix as to what should be their stand in this global confrontation. The British Raj was already feeling emaciated and the people in India begun to discuss the consequences.

"The British will be trounced!"

"But these Japanese are no better than them."

"Nevertheless, a foreigner is a foreigner!"

"Should we support the Govt. in this War?"

"We just can't neglect the Govt. Our Sardar (Patel) has clearly defined our stand. Unless we get an assurance of autonomy from the Govt., India would not be a party in this global confrontation."

"Only Sardar has this audacity to say so categorically... Not even Gandhi Ji is so clear!"

"But the source of our strength is only Gandhi Ji. In fact both Sardar and Bapu form the Congress's basic think-tank."

After some days the Viceroy declared India's siding with the Allied forces without even consulting the Central Assembly.

One of the Congress leaders commented: "This British Raj is not letting India rest in peace."

The other Congressman said: "History will teach him the lesson."

"But who will write our history with a clear-headed and impartial analysis?"

"Rest assured. Mr. Ramakant is writing history of this period."

"Hope he writes weighing all the pros and cons from the Congress's side as well," hoped a seasoned leader.

***

The whole country was now itching for freedom. From every corner of the country the sparks were flying and the Govt. was getting singed with the heat of the nationalist aspirations.

Earlier, on 6th June 1934 Sardar Patel had been chosen as the Chairperson of the Congress's Parliamentary Board. Its other members were Maulana Abul Kalaam Azad, Mahamana Madan Mohan Malviya, Rajindra Prasad and other stalwarts.

History bears testimony to the fact that what inspired the Indian youth then was a trident of three sentiments: Gandhi Ji's sacrifice, Sardar's firmness and the revolutionary spirit of Subhash Bose. The youth were charged with the fire of nationalism. The Congress was the main stream of nationalism with which were merging the streams of other parties as well. They might have different path but their destination was the same – India's Independence!

When the elections for the Central Assembly were held the Congress bagged 44 seats and when on 26th Jan. 1935 its session began, the Congressmen defeated the Govt. on many issues.

Meanwhile, the things took an adverse turn in Gujarat. In fact Borsad had suffered the plague epidemic. By 1935 it spread to 27 adjoining villages. People were greatly distressed. Since the Govt. was rather indifferent, it was Sardar Patel who inspired people to help each other. The Govt. officials were showing a crass callousness. Sardar Patel himself created a team of the volunteers and without any aid from the Govt. a hospital was opened in Borsad's cantonment area. After some time Sardar himself came there to run the hospital's administration. With the help of his team of volunteer and doctors who joined the hospital out of their nationalist zeal, a grim battle was raged against that deadly plague. With the result they could eliminate this menace totally.

But in the political arena the centre of discussion was to prepare the Constitution of India. In July 1935, one Govt. of India Act was promulgated according to which some States were given independent status and it was decided to create a federal body. At this time Dr. Rajindra Prasad was chosen as the Congress President. It was under his leadership that the Congress decided to participate in the Assembly elections. In 1936 the Congress session was held under Jawahar Lal Nehru's presidentship. It was decided then that the Congress would also participate in the State Assembly elections.

Sardar Patel had always been associated with his grassroot level. He loved to do something solid and hence he was associated with many public institutions. In March 1935 he attended the convocation of the Gurukul Kangri (a famous indigenous educational institute). While returning from there he was afflicted with pneumonia. And despite the doctor's opposition he went to attend the Congress Session in Lucknow.

After two months of the session, the Congress' one stalwart, Dr. Ansari expired and Sardar Patel was chosen as the Chairperson of the Congress's Parliamentary Board. In the ensuing meeting of the Board, the names of the Congress candidates for the imminent election were announced. In August 1936, in a vital meeting of the Congress, its Election Manifesto was also discussed, finalized and eventually accepted with the strategy prepared for the elections.

It was clearly a very hectic period for Sardar Patel. His popularity was growing with a tremendous pace which was natural as he knew the causes that ailed the common men. He had realized that mere word-play and sophistry couldn't alter the miserable condition of the people. The freedom to implement the party's decision was not tentamount to removing the common men's problems – it was just the step. And he had displayed such sincerity by his role in the previous agitations. His firm commitment to ensure public welfare made his popularity touch the pinnacle during this phase.

But like the drop of water on the pinnacle, the popularity doesn't stay for long at the highest point. At times even one's well-wishers commit such acts as make it plummet. A similar event occurred soon. In 1936, it was decided that the next session of the Congress would be held in Faizpur (Maharashtra) in which Sardar Patel was to remain saddled with the President's post. But all were aghast when it was declared that on Gandhi's advice Patel withdrew his name and instead proposed the name of Pt. Jawahar Lal Nehru.

Addressing the session Patel said: "Even though I have withdrawn my name, it doesn't mean that I toe Jawahar Lal Ji's line. Our Congressmen know well that we have differences on certain important issues!" This way he made it clear that for the sake of the Party's unity he had withdrawn his name from the race of the party presidentship and not because he accepted what the other section wanted. He didn't care any dent on his personal popularity if the party's unity remained unscathed. He also wanted to impress upon the fellow members that the Congress Party was truly a democratic party in which dissension didn't mean personal enmity. He also urged the party men to provide whole hearted support to Pt. Nehru who – he said – 'at present the right man to guide the party.'

Patel's this speech disappointed many of his supporters and well-wishers who wanted him to become the President. They had a heated argument with Patel:

"Sardar! This wasn't a wise step. You should have resisted Bapu's this decision by conveying our views. We don't doubt Pundit Ji's (Nehru's) ability or sincerity but at present we need an Iron Man."

"I shall work to that end still. But you know, a contest between Nehru and me would have created a chasm in our ranks. Gandhi Ji said we shouldn't let the Govt. get such an opportunity."

"But Nehru's knowledge of political nuances is confined to just three provinces while you know most of the country," argued one man.

"So what! He would know! We're there to help him. Moreover, you all must also start believing your leader," advised Sardar, "like I do my Bapu, Gandhi Ji."

There are not many leaders even now who could be so loyal to their leader. Despite personal loss to his popularity, Patel did this sacrifice for the unity of the party.

But there were some of his followers who wanted to pursue the matter. In the evening when Sardar was alone in his chamber, they reached him.

"Yes! What can I do for you." He asked the five gentlemen who came in.

"We have strong objection to your address to the Party's session today."

"Why? What is the ground of your objection?"

"How you could give such an assurance on other's behalf?"

"What sort of assurance?"

"That Jawahar Lal Ji would accept the people's demands even though he might not personally agree with them?"

"That was my assessment. I know him. But I could say so openly because I am not enamoured of sticking to a power or position."

"You may not, but we do want you to occupy that position."

"Thank you! It is your this affection that has made me what I'm today."

"And still, you're trying to leave us in the lurch!"

"No! I have not left you in the lurch. But I have given you the leadership of someone quite competent. You know I couldn't have gone against Bapu."

"No one can go against Bapu. He is a father-figure for most of us. But one thing I may tell you, Sardar. I am an expert astrologer!" said one of them.

"So what your astrology predicts for the country?" asked Sardar.

"With Jawahar Lal Ji leading the country, he may have to face many problems due to his rather indecisive nature."

"And what does my horoscope say?"

"It says that you'll have to do a lot of sacrifices. That is your destiny."

"Then you all should realize it. And shed your anger at my to-day's decision," Sardar said with his enigmatic smile.

"But there is also one very vital aspect of your destiny, which I must tell you."

"What's that?"

"It says that you will be a nation-builder."

"Then also you all shouldn't worry!"

"But you'll have to face much opposition."

And this way the people continued to come to him and Sardar Patel explained him the very cause of his that day's speech!

Things moved ahead with their natural pace. In Feb. 1937 State Assembly Elections were held as scheduled. The Congress got clear majority in UP, Madras (modern Tamilnadu), Bihar and Orissa and in Bombay, Bengal and in NWFP. It emerged as the largest party. Only in Sindh and Punjab it received comparatively less number of votes.

Now the biggest job at hand was choosing the leaders for the State Assemblies, forming the cabinet and making it work with the British Raj's Administration. That complicated and intriguing process was sure to create dissension. It started in Bombay Assembly:

"I should have been the winner," complained K.F. Nariman.

"Then how it didn't come to pass?" asked other leaders.

"Bal Gangadhar Kher has been elected instead. How?"

"It must be the conspiring move of Patel."

"But Patel doesn't indulge in conspiracies. He never indulges in such lowly manipulations."

"I'll raise this issue in the Congress' Working Committee meeting."

"We will demand an enquiry."

The enquiry was made by a Parsi Judge, D. N. Bahadur who judged all such charges to be totally baseless.

Now the events began to happen in a fast pace. The winning parties were invariably pitted against the Governors in various State. The Governors were requested that if they promised in writing about not using their prerogatives, the Congress might come ahead to form its cabinet.

On 20th March 1937 the Governors invited the Congress to form its cabinet in six states, though without promising anything beforehand. The Congress was disturbed at this 'double standard' policy of the British Raj and between 26th – 27th March it flatly refused to form its cabinet in any of the States.

With the result in U.P. and Bihar the minority parties formed their cabinet.

The resoluteness of the Congress earned wide approval of the Congress workers. They Bailed it as a 'most befitting stand against the dishonest Govt."

"That will happen when we have Gandhi Ji like patient leader and Patel like faithful follower. They shall teach this unfair Govt. a bitter lesson."

The Congress' this widely approved decision received Kudoes from all over the country. Even in London, some free thinking political leaders supported the Indian National Congress on this point. This uproarious support forced the Viceroy to make an open declaration: "In prerogatives of the Governors are their constitutional right only, they can't be used practically to over rule the chosen representatives."

The very next day the Viceroy had to explain it publicly. The Govt. realized that mere reiteration of its plans would not be sufficient. It had to implement them or at least show its true intention of putting them to practice.

On 7th July, the Congress Working Committee held its special meeting and it was decided that since the Viceroy's this declaration met its conditions, this party would form its cabinet in the States.

At last things became amicable between the Viceroy and the Congress Cabinet and the minority governments had to resign. Pt. Govinda Ballabh Pant in U. P., Shree Krishna Singh in Bihar, Rajgopalacharis in Madras, Dr. N. B. Khare in M.P., Balgangadhar Kher in Bombay and Shree Vishwanath Das in Orissa formed their cabinets. In Assam the Congress leader Bardolai moved a no confidence motion against Sir Mohammed Sadullah's govt. which was passed and the Congress led govt. was also formed there. All these cabinets in various states started working under the direction of the Congress Parliamentary Board President, Sardar Patel.

Following these Congress cabinets in various states, the pieces of land of the farmers that were forefeited during the Satyagraha agitation were returned to them. The farmers felt delighted. They felt immensely pleased with Sardar.

"This is all the doings of our beloved Sardar!"

"Sardar is truly great. If he wanted he could have become Bombay's Chief Minsiter."

"Huh! Chief Minister," said the other, "Parliamentary Board's President is much bigger than that."

It was on Sardar Patel's advice that the Congress' next session took place in Bardoli's one sector Iripura in 1938. As the President of the Congress' Parliamentary Board Sardar did many important works.

He had to solve many problems that kept on arising between the Congress leaders in various states. But he had a very unique way of solving them. One such example was the factionalism in M.P. cabinet led by Dr. Khare with the other faction having the tussle, led by Ravi Shankar Shukla and Dwarika Prasad Misra. Patel asked Dr. Khare to resign but he refused. Then he asked the two minister's Shukla and Misra; they also refused to oblige him. At last he advisded the Governor to dissolve the Assembly of the state. Sardar never felt any hitch in taking even the hardest decision if he felt it necessary for the party and eventually for the country. His hard decision in M.P.'s politics received thundering approval from Pt. Nehru and other top leaders.

When the state governments received the benefit of the autonomy, their appetite for total independence grew manifold. Even the royal families of the State were itching for redemption from the British rule. This demand grew so intense that by 1938-39 agitations began in many princely states as the public began to demand responsible administration.

Patel himself led many agitation in South India. Many a time the situation became so dangerous that even his life was in peril but undaunted, he kept on doing his job. As the President of the Congress Parliamentary Party he added many feathers to his cap. But although the agitations within the princely states for self rule failed, these protests help Sardar a lot when later he made these dynasties merge their existence in the Indian Union.

The various Congress governments in different states took a major step of ensuring release of the armed revolutionaries. Patel had a soft corner for them. He always called them 'the right persons on the wrong path!' Although the Governors of the State were against the release of the imprisoned revolutionaries, Patel stood firm on his ground. Initially even the Bihar and UP govt. had to resign on this issue but after some time the governors softened their stands and the Congress cabinet was restored in the two states. It was Patel's idea to have the revolutionaries released.

In fact the basic problem in the Administration was that despite the procedures were laid down according to the 1935 Govt. of India Act, yet the projects were formed on the basis of the 1919 Act. Hence there was much confusion. With the result, the tussle between the Congress and the British Raj continued. But the country had to wait for their solution for at least a decade more.

***

The cycle of the political events in the country moved with quite a fast pace. But the situation drastically altered with the outbreak of the Second World War whose main arena became Europe with Britain becoming one of the main participants.

"Did you read the Viceroy's declaration?" Patel asked Mahadeva Bhai.

"Yes, read and pondered over it also?"

"There wasn't much to ponder over," replied Patel. "It is a straightforward declaration. Indian soldiers will fight for Britain. Our sacrifice will ensure their victory!"

"And suppose Britain fails to win. Will then the British leave India?"

"Then we might have the Japanese – German rule."

"Not necessary."

"Look at their victory in Burma!"

"That is only a minor triumph."

"But in the event of the British leaving India, will we be able to handle our independence?" asked Jawahar Lal Nehru who also reached there suddenly.

"Have confidence, Jawahar," Patel said keeping his hand on Nehru Ji's shoulder.

"I have confidence. But what about the serious of minor rulers raising their head in the power vacuum?" Nehru indicated towards a series eventuality.

"This is quite a possibility," opined Mahadev Bhai.

"That's why I say Viceroy's declaration is a cunning move made by the British," Patel said. "When we asked for our rule they have indicated the presence of other claimants as well. It is very much clear in the Declaration."

"No doubt, the declaration is quite intriguing." Nehru admitted.

"But the intention is apparent. It says: 'Britain wants to give India colonial self-rule. After the end of this War, with everybody's consent the 1935 Constitution will be suitably modified."

"What's wrong in that," Mahadeva Bhai said.

"Everything. All those at least some of them raising their head, then may also dance to the tune of the Indian Muslim League."

"We will try to win people's favour," declared Patel.

While this discussion was on, the then Congress President Rajendra Prasad gave his statement, calling the Viceroy's declaration as quite disappointing. Dr. Prasad even appealed to all the Congress Cabinets in the States to tender their resignation.

The Congress was rather confused about its course of action. A CWC (Congress Working Committee) session was hurriedly called at Wardha. It was here that Sardar's position acquired added significance. But before delibering his speech he thought it prudent to consult his close friends.

"This is a difficult situation. I don't know how to go about it." Patel asked.

"Don't worry. Keep on trying the best way that you think."

"I don't think we can talk on the conditions put forth by the Muslim League."

"But you must start the process."

"According to me there is one option."

"Which one?"

"We must demand from the Govt. the Constitution prepared by the people's representatives."

"We don't think the Govt. would accept it."

"Then we can also continue our non-cooperation."

And amidst these 'ifs' and 'buts' Sardar delivered his speech:

"We are invariably and repeatedly asked– 'Are we ready to receive Independence?' We are also advised that we must end our differences with the Muslim League. But we know that these are the techniques of procrastination. Once we do this, then we will be advised to settle our disputes with the princely states. And even if this is done we shall be asked: 'What would happen to the Europeans in India who have many projects going on in India?' They have many vested interests as well. The Englishmen always say that God has sent them to look after all the rival forces operating in India so as to keep land-mass united. But we say let us have our Constitution prepared by our people's representatives. If they accept our this request we may start our negotiations with the Muslim League."

His speech had a mixed response among the people:

"Sardar has given a very deep-meaningful speech."

"I think it is a very timely demand."

"An inherent attempt to find a via media to have an agreement with our representatives," summarized a Muslim participant.

"What kind of agreement you refer to?"

"How can I clarify? It is yet to be reached between the Congress and the Muslim League."

"You know the purpose of the Muslim League's existence?"

"Apparently to protect Muslims' interest and actually to create for itself some space in India's political firmament."

"This is actually a down-right divisive purpose," commented a nationalist Muslim. "At present our purpose should be throwing out the British through our united efforts. We can have our share in the Independence once it is achieved and the Britishers leave our shore."

"No!" said a diehard Muslim, "It has to be decided beforehand. Once the difference is created it is never removed. Have the Shia's and Sunni's been able to remove their differences? Riots between them keep on taking place. Even time has failed to remove the differences between them."

Then a senior man opined: "Well. Leave these issues for the leaders dear! Let them decide. Ultimately it is God's will that will prevail. So why waste your energy on these matters? For we the common men arranging just two meals a day is a great problem. Let us try to find its solution first."

***

But the Viceroy refused let the people's Constitution prevail. And his refusal threw a gauntlet before the Congress once again.

On 10th Jan. 1940 the declaration was made for the approval of the Colonial Rule but the Congress refused to accept it. It demanded complete freedom. Gandhi Ji (now famously called Mahatma Gandhi; the 'Mahatma' epithet was given to him by Ravindra Nath Tagore) had option go but to start his Satyagraha. Although this approach was acceptable to most of the Congressmen, there were some, who found this to be a hackneyed approach, and they started to toy even with the idea of creating a separate party for themselves.

Meanwhile, the scene at the international screen was acquiring grim images as Germany was scoring a series of victories over the Allied Forces.

At home, the Congress started its demand for the total freedom through a Satyagraha whose leader was Abul Kalaam Azad, chosen specially to dilute the very base of the Muslim League's demand.

The British faced this double wham: agitation within and a full fledged War without!

In April 1940 Holland fell followed by Norway and Denmark's surrender before the German might. Not only this the redoubtable France was also brought to its knees by the German forces on 14th June. This was the front news that was disturbing but not much disparaging. However with the defeat of the English forces at Hukark changed the entire scenario for the UK strategy. Prime Minister Chamberlain resigned and Churchill was sworn in as the new PM at the 'Worst possible moment, on the worst possible ground' (to use Churchill's own description of the time he was sworn in). Churchill did a lot to raise up the sagging morale of the British people by his fiery speeches and invocations.

In order to resolve the political crises in India Lord Emry was made Minister for India. In the British Parliament, he reiterated the offer for Colonial rule in India.

The Viceroy invited the Indian leaders for talks in Shimla – the summer capital of India then. Gandhi Ji, Patel, Nehru and other leaders reached Shimla. They had to resolve the two basic issues.

- In what proportion the members of the Viceroy's Executive Council should be enhanced.
- The proposal for creating an all party government in Delhi was revived and accepted and the same was to accepted by the Viceroy.

But the results of the Shimla Conference were disappointing. The Congress decided to review the point in its Poona session to be held on 27th July.

However, the disturbing trend was the leaders' mutual differences began to surface at an alarming pace. Patel was asked about then by his friends.

But reassuring then Sardar said: "Don't worry. Everything will be done with justice and in proper manner."

"But you may be asked to back track. That you should not accept."

"Well! Don't misjudge the other people. They may have different approach but our aim is the same."

"It means you may accept whatever they say."

"I am a disciplined soldier of the party. I can't disobey my leader."

In order to pacify his followers' frayed temper, Sardar gave them a lecture.

"You all will read whatever our Bapu has written. He says that 'Sardar will have to back track'. But how can I back track when I have not moved forward. I have told him that if he allows me to follow him I shall do it blindly. But it appears he doesn't want me to even follow him. Nevertheless, no one can and should defy Gandhi Ji. I shall do what he says."

Although Sardar tried to hide his feelings, it was apparent to his close associates like Rajendra Prasad and Acharya Kripalini that Sardar was going through some severe tension. They discussed the matter between themselves.

"You're tense, Sardar," asked Kripalani, "What is the reason?"

"I'm tense because of the difference between the approaches of Jawahar and Bapu. That is not good for our party and country, both."

"That is there. But soon we'd find some way to reconcile their view points."

"Suppose the British decide to leave suddenly!" Changing the unpleasant topic Sardar tossed up his wish.

"Then there might be great Chaos." Kripalani was apprehensive.

"Nothing of the sort will happen!" Sardar assured.

"Don't forget, Sardar, that there are many princely states… they may claim their independence as well."

"Oh! That is not a worry. I'll set them right in a week's time."

"You're either joking or over confident," Kriplani said.

"I assure you that I say this all with a careful thought. I'll make them join our Indian union in one thread."

"Sardar! You are over-presumptuous! These princely states have their chequered history. They won't agree so easily."

"It will happen. Don't underestimate our Army!"

"But the Constitutional provisions?"

"We will see to that too. Don't worry for those states. We won't be needing force at all. Trust my tactics."

Then they had the discussion about the War!

"What are the Japanese's plans?"

"We'd know in a fortnight."

"Will the change in Britain's leadership impact on our politics?"

"But it is heard that Subhash is siding with the Japanese forces. Won't that will help us?"

"Dear Acharya Ji, the situation at present is quite fluid. Nevertheless we all want the Englishmen sent back to their land. Even Bapu also concurs on this point. It is Jawahar who wants no heart burning between us and the Englishmen." Patel concluded.

"Perhaps he is not far wrong. It is better we part as friends." Kripalani opined.

As the coincidence would have it, Jawahar Lal Ji happened to reach there and said: "What are you discussing, brothers?"

Patel said: "Jawahar, you know what we generally discuss nowadays. We were discussing options available to gain our objective."

"But we have different approaches. While Gandhi Ji has different view-point, I have also a different approach. And yours is a class apart."

"Only if we could have a single approach," said Kripalani, "Then we may have a greater punch in our contention."

"No Acharya Ji!" Pt. Nehru said emphatically, "Ours is a democratic party. Like India we also represent unity in diversity."

At that point Maulana Azad came in and said: “According to the UK newspapers, Churchill is not as much troubled by the ongoing war as by Gandhi Ji’s moves.”

“He knows how to fight with weapons,” Patel said with a smile, “but he has no idea how to battle with morals and sacrifices.”

“You know,” Nehru Ji said. “He wanted the Viceroy to suppress our agitations with naked force but the latter refused to toe his PM’s line. Our Viceroy respects our Bapu. He knows that all world-leaders like even President Roosevelt calls him a ‘Saint Faqeer’. But I don’t know why our Viceroy fails to agree to what our Bapu says.”

Patel said with a smile: “You must impress on him, Jawahar, that Bapu’s way is the only way. Ask him not to worry about the possible communal riots. We will manage like the Christians manges the Catholic and Protestant tussles.”

This way the top leaders continued their discussions to find a unified way to oust the British from India. It was the consequence of these confabulations that Gandhi Ji met the Viceroy almost daily between 27th to 30th Dec. But no result could emerge finally.

Now the question emerged: “What should the Congress do?”

“Satyagraha is the only option left with us,” Gandhi Ji said.

“But they’d try to crush it,” said Sardar.

“That we are prepared for. Gold needs to pass through fire to become more radiant,” said Gandhi Ji.

So the Congress decided to stage yet another Satyagraha. This time Gandhi Ji with the party's consent chose first Vinoba Bhave as its leader. Gandhi Ji spoke against India's participation in the War. Govt. was miffed and put censor on all his speeches publication. But Gandhi kept on addressing the people. On 21st October he was arrested. Then Nehru was chosen as the leader of the peaceful agitation. But on 31st October he was also imprisoned.

Sardar Patel was leading the agitation in Gujarat. On 17th Nov. 1940 he spoke in a public meeting criticizing the India's participation in the War. He was warned by the Govt. but he didn't stop. At last on 18th Nov. 1940 he was arrested in the night. Many other stalwarts were also arrested. Following his arrest Sardar was kept in the Sabarmati Jail. But he developed high fever the very next day. For about 4 days his fever remained high, at times touching 104 F. Then he was shifted to the Yervada prison. There also his illness remained uncured. The Govt. physicians advised a surgical operation immediately. At last in August 1941 he was released. He then consulted his private physicians. Sardar was against the surgical operation. At last he went to Wardha Ashram near Gandhi Ji where he became better with natural therapy treatment.

When he felt better he went to Bardoli. Meanwhile by the 1st week of Dec. 1941 all the arrested members of the Congress Working Committee were released. As they were released they assembled at Borivilli and held an impromptu meeting of the Congress Working Committee. Here some of the CWC members developed some differences with Gandhi Ji on the form of Satyagraha. Gandhi Ji felt so isolated that he said: "The Congress Committees may act in any way in self-defence." Indicating his view on this issue he wrote in his paper 'Harijan' on 14th March 1942: "If the soldiers maltreat the women they should face the oppressor any way they deem fit, even by resorting to violence. My non-violence means non-violence of the brave, not the cowardice of the timid."

But the Govt. in Britain was quite conscious of the turbulence occurring in India. On 23rd March 1942, it sent a mission to India under the leadership of Sir Stufford Cripps (popularly known as the Cripps Mission) with a definite plan for India's independence. All the top leaders of the political parties were invited in Delhi to ponder over this plan. Sardar also went to Delhi. The salient points of this plan, briefly, were the following:

- Soon India will be granted colonial autonomy.
- At the end of the World War II the Constituent Assembly will be constituted with the participation and consent of all the main political parties of India.
- First the Provincial Assembly elections will be held and they will conduct the Constituent Assembly Elections.
- In proportion to the total population of the country, the princely states will also be allowed to send their representatives in the Constituent Assembly.
- Every princely state will have an option to merge or not merge with the Indian Union and their agreements with the British Govt. will be honoured. The Constituent Assembly will also give its commitment to honouring such agreements.

- During the War period the Indian Army will remain under the control of the British Government while other Departments will be controlled by the Indians.

The Congress Working Committee held its special session thrice to consider the Cripps proposals which were eventually rejected by it. Its main objection was for the proposal connected to defence. Sir Cripps sent an invitation to Gandhi Ji. At last the British Govt. accepted the amendment in the defence proposal that an Indian would also be part of the War Committee. The proposal of the ca binet status to all the members of the Viceroy's executive council was eventually rejected.

By this time fighting on the side of the Axis Powers, Japan, had captured Hongkong, Singapore, Malaya and other islands, forcing their citizen leave their abodes as the refugees. They sought shelter in India. In order to consider their influx into India, the Congress held its meeting in Allahabad in April 1942. But it found no relief in the Cripps Mission.

Meanwhile, taking advantage of the Govt.'s engagement with the on going War, the Muslim League emphatically demanded its share – formation of Pakistan. Curiously enough, Rajgopalachari was even prepared to concede it. But as the Chairperson of the Congress's Parliamentary Board, Sardar Patel opposed it and demanded Rajgopalachari's explanation. This difference became so incisive that Rajgopalachari even resigned from the CWC. But in the Allahabad session his resignation was not accepted.

It was in the Allahabad session that Gandhi Ji gave his slogan: "Britishers, Quit India!" He had decided to start an agitation with the same slogan. The Congress accepted it.

While addressing a huge public rally, on 26th July 1942, Sardar Patel explained to the people as to what this Quit India Movement meant. He said: "You should not fear that at the age of 74 Gandhi Ji will be left alone. We all are together in it. This movement enshrines the essence of our movements that we launched right after the Rowlatt Act of 1919. We want Indians to resign their Govt. jobs, leave their present occupation to isolate the Britishers so that they could leave the country without any hitch. We invoke all Indians to unite and throw these foreigners out of our country. But we want no violence. We want these foreigners to leave India on their own, willingly and peacefully. This is the time when you have to do your part in ensuring your country's freedom."

Sardar Patel also addressed a journalists conference on 28th July in Ahmedabad followed by his fiery address to the students at the same venue the very next day. After addressing a women's rally on 30th he went to Bombay and delivered his famous speech in August 1942 at Chowapaati: He said: "…this war is to be fought by you all as soon Gandhi Ji and other leaders will be arrested. We have already enlightened you about how this agitation should be continued. But never be violent or cause any disturbance in the city life. So come forward for ensuring freedom to our motherland…! Let nothing obstruct your way…!"

On 7th & 8th August the Congress held its meeting in Bombay, Supporting Gandhi Ji's 'Quit India Movement', Patel said: "Our main weapon is non-violence. No matter what provocations are made, we must stick to our this weapon. No matter we all are arrested, we must make our countrymen fight it out the same way. It is not only our movement but it is chiefly people's movement. We are the trigger while they are the explosion. We know that including our chief commander (Gandhi Ji) all of us will be arrested on flimsy grounds. But this Movement shouldn't stop before the British are sent back to where they belong!"

Sardar's these sentiments received total support from Maulana Azad, Pt. Nehru and other stalwarts. Before the Viceroy could be informed about this agitation, the Administration disconnected all the telephones of the top leaders. On 9th April at 4 a.m. all the CWC members including Sardar Patel, were arrested. Gandhi Ji was also arrested. But before being imprisoned, Gandhi Ji told all Indians: "It is about time... Do or Die!"

Sardar Patel was arrested from his residence, 68 Marine Drive where he was staying with his daughter Maniben and the Congress General Secretary, Acharya J.B. Kripalani. Maniben was also arrested and sent to Yervada jail with other arrested ladies including Sarojini Naidu.

For about three months Patel had no contact with the outside world. He had good company in the jail as Pt. Nehru, Azad, and Dr. Sayyad Mehmood were there. Pt. Nehru completed his famous book 'Discovery of India' while imprisoned here. In that jail, Patel learnt that some of the top Congress leaders were not happy with Gandhi Ji's launching this movement. Their argument was that this slogan (British! Quit India!) was in a bad taste and Indian leaders might lose their sympathy of their foreign well-wishers (like the USA and its protege Chiang Kai Shek). But Patel countered their argument by supporting Gandhi Ji whole heartedly saying: "It is a direct way of seeking our freedom and ensuring emancipation from the foreign rule."

In this jail these top leaders of the Congress had enough time to exchange their notes. Patel studied Gita and other books. However, be couldn't maintain good health as mostly he was ill.

At times he felt as though his end was near! But he kept on doing what he deemed proper even during his illness. On 11th August he received a tragic news that his old friend Mahadeva Desai had passed away. He was quite heart-broken, and during this phase he lost his weight alarmingly.

When Sardar Patel was in jail, his son, Dahyabai was free and his job was to distribute the copies of the speeches delivered by Bapu Ji (Gandhi Ji), his father and other leaders. But on 19th Nov. 1942 he was also arrested. Dahyabai and his sister, Maniben were kept imprisoned by the Govt. without filing any case against them.

With the arrest of the top leaders, the British Govt. grew all the more vindictive. It had arrested all those who could cause it any inconvenience. Censor was imposed on newspapers. Its reckless measures were responded by as intensive revolt by the people. Communication-lines were disrupted, many post-offices, telegraph offices and stations were burned. This fire reached the villages as well. The people's rebuff to the Govt.'s reckless oppression almost paralysed all normal activities in the country.

Against the Govt.'s repressive and cruel measures, Gandhi Ji wrote a letter to the Viceroy. When his letter remained unresponded, from 10th Jan. he began to keep fast. At that time he was under house-arrest in the Agha Khan Palace in Poona. Some leaders wrote a combined letter requesting release of ailing Gandhi Ji but their efforts bore no fruit.

It was precisely the period when Bengal faced a severe famine, killing thousands of person out of sheer starvation. On 6th May 1942, Gandhi Ji, severely ill, was eventually released. Sardar Patel was still in Ahmedanagar Jail. After Gandhi's release he could establish correspondence with him. Although his letters were opened by the British authority, he used to write in a coded language to give the needed information clandestinely to the addressed person. Looking at the international arena, he realized that willy or nilly Britain would have to grant India independence. Hence he thought not much sense left in a continued struggle with the Govt.

But Gandhi Ji's release was greeted with yet another unexpected development. Muslim League was now adamant to have its Pakistan. Rajagopalachari arranged a meeting between the Muslim League and the Congress leaders to sort out the Hindu-Muslim unity issue. On 9th Sept. Gandhi Ji met Mohd. Ali Jinnah and they kept on meeting for 19 days at a stretch but nothing tangible could be achieved due to Jinnah's intransigence.

In 1945 Lord Wavel came as Viceroy of India. He was impressed with Gandhi's magnanimous personality. Meeting him again, he wrote to English PM that there was room of agreement in the imminent transfer of power in the sub-continent. But Jinnah claimed that he never wanted to get 'a dilapidated and moth-eaten Pakistan'.

Gandhi Ji was against India's division yet he had differences with his lieutenants like Nehru and Patel and many others. The topic was discussed threadbare. On 21st June 1945 in the meeting of Congress Working Committee:

"No! Pakistan should not be created." Gandhi Ji said.

"But Jinnah is adamant!" Patel responded.

"Make Jinnah the Prime Minister of the undivided India to make him accept what we say," Gandhi Ji suggested.

"But the problem between our Party and the Muslim League may lead to many serious repercussions, still," Abul Kalaam declared.

"But I won't accept Jinnah as the PM of the free India." Nehru said with unconcealed asperity.

"Who'd you accept as the PM except your own self?" Patel said in a lighter vein.

"This is no time for jokes, Patel Bhai," Nehru requested.

"Okay. But how would you satisfy the demand for even participation in the Govt."

Patel had learnt from his friends that in the coming Shimla conference, despite being in minority, the Muslims would be accorded even representation.

"Could there be Muslims who aren't members of the Muslim League?"

"No! Muslim representation to only Muslim League members is what the British strategist may offer."

"And what about the progressive Muslims?" Abul Kalaam asked.

"Ask Patel Ji," Nehru said angrily.

But despite these discussion the unified stand didn't appear plausible. Most of the Congress-men relied on Patel's worldliwiseness to resolve this impasse. There was also a group in the Congress which was out and out leftist in thinking. Eventually it was expelled from the Congress in the Calcutta meeting of the Working Committee, in order to have a homogeneous, like-minded people's strong group.

The leftist believed in resorting to violence if the occasion demanded. Their argument was: "We believe in what our Subhash is doing. His Indian National Fauj has pulverized the British. We must use all the means available to throw out the foreigners. Only Satyagraha may not be effective."

The Congress could not become indifferent to Subhash and his army, the INA. When a committee was constituted to find out the INA soldiers killed in action, Patel became its Chairman. And he worked devotedly to find the details of these unknown 'martyrs' as he called them.

***

In the last phases of the 5th decade of the 20th century, in India, Patel was deemed to be the problem-solver for both, the Govt. and the Congress. When the thinking seemed to go out of control Patel was asked to put the things in order. And that methodical Iron-Man had an unusual knack to create order out of any chaos. Gandhi Ji knew his quality well. He had an immense faith in the administrative qualities of his chief assistant.

In 1946, in the very beginning itself the Naval forces – chiefly the Indians revolted in Bombay port. In their support all the navy officers in Madras, Karachi, Calcutta port went on strike. Even the Royal Air Force officers did the same. It was akin to a major rebellion by the defence forces, barring the Army. Now the people became quite scared, especially those who believed in the might of the British Empire.

"A revolt by the naval forces bodes ill for the Empire."

"What has been the cause?"

"Clearly the discrimination showed to the white officers." You can't practice such a blatant discrimination on the basis of the colour of skin. After all, they all serve the king with equal dedication. Now the British officers have their days numbered in this part of the world."

"Now even the white skinned officers are fearful. They have refused to go to the actual site of strike."

When the news and the public unrest reached the Congress leaders, Kripalani said in a jocular vein. "I think only Sardar can do something to restore normally."

The Govt. as if heard Kripalani's this suggestion. Sardar was actually approached by the Govt. agencies to have this strike taken off. But Sardar put forth his conditions:

"The Govt. must ensure that no punishment will be given to the strikers."

"Accepted!"

"Even financially no one would be punished – no cut in their salary – allowance etc."

"It has already been accepted."

Then Sardar went to meet the strikers. They complained: "We have been suffering this balant discrimination for a long time."

"Now no discrimination will be made."

"What's the guarantee?"

"Well, you know, they are already shaky in their position in our country."

"That's the reason they sent you instead of coming themselves."

"You may interpret it as you want. But this strike must be called off."

"We believe your words. Because soon you will be guiding the country."

As this strike was called off immediately, that by the postal department went on strike. Again Sardar was called to intervene. And in no time he did the needful.

But Sardar's all these achievements created much jealousy in the heart of some of his colleagues in the Party who wanted to create a wedge between Pt. Nehru and Patel so as to derive greater importance for themselves.

***

Now Britain was sending a series of the delegations in order to learn more about the conditions prevailing in India. Even when the postal department strike in the was continuing there was a British delegation touring India.

On 23rd March 1946 a delegation called 'Cabinet Mission' reached India. It was assigned a task to arrange for the Cabinet formation in India. It had three members. Lord Pattick, the India Minister, Atford Cripps and A.B. Alexander. They did not want India's division but Jinnah's adamant behavior created much problem for them. He wanted India's division and carving out Pakistan from it. Even when they talked to the Muslim League, it didn't budge from its stand an inch.

The Cabinet Mission issued many proposals but Sardar Patel summarily rejected all of them, saying: "Those proposals would divide India into pieces and hence totally unacceptable."

Some of the salient points of the proposal are given below:

- Defence and foreign affairs may remain under the centre's control. The centre may remain empowered to levy taxes in order to get the funds for meeting their expense.
- An Indian Union may be created containing the British India and the Princely States.
- The rest of the subjects – barring foreign affairs and defence – may remain with the Provinces.
- The Indian Union may have the representatives from the British India and the princely states.
- The Political parties may have the right to create their Assemblies and send their representatives in them.
- The review of the constitutional provision may be done after a decade.
- The Provincial Assembly members may contribute in electing the members of the Constituent Assembly. For this, one people's representative may be created from a million population. Every community may be free to elect its representative.
- A temporary Govt. may be immediately constituted in the centre.

Obviously these proposals were bound to divide India all the more, not only on the regional but even the religious and communal basis. Hence these were rejected by Sardar Patel.

It was a coincidence that the Indian Congress also held its internal elections at this time only. While Pt. Nehru was elected President, Patel was chosen to be the treasurer of the Party.

With the above mentioned proposals fanning the communal divide, the Muslim League started dreaming the days when their community would rule over entire India. They started provocations which were resisted by the other communities and this trend led to blood-shed and riots in some area.

Patel was the Home Minister of the Interim Government and he was a worried man, getting the news of communal flare up from almost all parts of the country.

His one friend gave him a new paper full of the gory details of the riots, and asked: "Sardar! What is this? The communal fire spreading fast!"

"I think this was bound to happen. Now let me see what Dr. Khan does?"

"What do you expect him to do?"

"To cheek the Hindus and Muslims.... But how?"

"Riots are the creation of the Muslim League."

"Of course... but...?"

"But what?"

"The role of RSS...?"

"That is just a reaction!"

"It is... but highly objectionable at the same time!"

"It is a reaction. If the action is violent, how can the reaction be non-violent?"

Then Patel's friend drew his attention to a more disturbing news...

"See... This is a more diabolical news...?"

"Which one?"

"The iniquities perpetrated by the Suharawardy Govt.!"

"It is totally unacceptable!"

"And this statement of Pheroz Khan!"

"Read it out to me."

"Muslims here will create such conditions as were created when Changez Khan and Halaku invaded India!"

Sardar remained speechless for a few moments.

"Why are you quiet?" asked his friend.

"Contemplation before doing any action is always advisable."

"What action do you envisage?"

"Guiding the gullible on the right path and punishing the incorrigible bigots."

Things had become alarmingly unbearable. It appeared as if some of the communities might never co-exist as they did in the past. It was in these inflammable conditions that the Congress held its session in Meerut.

A conversation between two members:

"What are you saying Kidwai?"

"This is what I feel!"

"No! You are wrong!"

"But Patel's speech in the session the other day?"

"No… that is impossible."

"You see the speech of Patel was against Jinnah's Muslim League based thinking and not against the Muslims in general!"

"But do you have any evidence to prove it?"

"Didn't he put a ban on the RSS?"

"That could be a political move as well!"

"Well... this is quite unfair... speaking against the RSS is right but against the League is wrong! How?"

"Communal thinking has polluted your mind!"

"As if only you're free from it. Look at the Muslim Congressmen – they want facilities. If they get them they are honoured citizens but if they oppose they are held as communal Muslims!"

"What is Gandhi's opinion on these developments?"

"He neither fully agrees with Patel nor totally rejects his opinions!"

"He is helplessly sandwiched between the two!"

"Not helpless because he believes Patel to be straightforward and honest."

Meanwhile, the British PM Lord Atlee, declared in the House of Commons that by June 1948 India would receive the total power. In March, 1947 Lord Mountbatten was sent as the new Viceroy of India to expedite the process of transfer of power from British Crown to Indian Union.

The news was received with misgivings and merriment together. A major change was about to occur. The imminent Independence created the thrill of getting the ultimate success but the ensuring law and order situation also created some serious trepidations. What would be the locus stands of the princely states in the new rule? Would the country be fragmented into pieces or would it remain one piece? These vital questions covered the country's firmament with uncertainty and chaos, yet with happiness and a sense of fulfillment also.

"Oh... brother! Did you hear the latest declaration from the British PM?"

"What?"

"It has been said that the Indian Constituent Assembly must come up with some 'all-acceptable constitution', or else…?"

"Else if this is not done the British Crown would give the power to rule to the Central Government or Present Provincial Government or the various princely states and shall cease to be the ruling authority in India…!"

People were exchanging their notes and showing each other the various interpretations of the British Crown. Unrest, chaos and uncertainty was writ large on their faces. All were out of their wits.

This uncertainty created many diabolical consequences. The communal passions were aroused with a murderous mood. The Muslim Leagues instigated riots in the NWFP regions. The Sikh and Hindus began to run out of their homes for shelter.

The riot's flame also engulfed Punjab. On 4th March 1947 the Hindu and Sikh demonstrators staged a Dharana in Lahore against the League's demand of Pakistan. It was just a peaceful demonstration with no trace of violence. In fact it was staged to protest against the riots but the Muslim League's agents aggressively attached the Hindu and Sikh demonstrations. Then all over Punjab – in Multan, Lahore etc. – the communal hatred spreaded quickly! The gory and beastly details of massacre in these parts began to rouse vengeance in rest of the region.

On 14th March, 1947 Pt. Nehru visited Punjab to assess the situation. He proposed to have three divisions of Punjab. In fact the situation had become so uncontrollable that in order to solve this communal hatred, Pt. Nehru and Patel were forced to accept the division of India.

On 24th March, Lord Mountbatten was appointed as the final Viceroy of India. With in two days of his assuming the charge he had a meeting with Gandhi Ji and Jinnah. After a day he again met Gandhi to reach a conclusive decision.

On 2nd May the Viceroy made it clear through his declaration that: "The Congress and the Muslim League have agreed for the division of India." He gave the order for division of Bengal and Punjab and constituting a commission to complete this job as early as possible.

The third point of the declaration said: 'Before affecting the division, these provinces' assembly members' opinion must also be sought.' It was clearly mentioned: 'The provinces willing for their division must elect their representatives for the Constituent Assembly in which the present representations won't be allowed. The Governor of the border-lying states will be changed and they will have the fresh elections conducted in due time.'

With the condition of the total transfer of power both the Muslim League and the Congress accepted this Declaration. On 14th June this declaration was pondered over in the Congress' major meeting and it was passed with 29 against and 153 votes favouring this division. Thirty six members remained neutral. At last Gandhi Ji also accepted this division of India which appeared inevitable. The Muslim League also gave its consent, and the representatives of the Sikhs also favoured it.

According to this transfer of power plan on 15th August Britain would handover power of rule to India and Pakistan.

Explaining his reasons for accepting the division of India, Patel said, later – after Independence – while justifying the stand: "I finally accepted the division of India when there was a possibility of losing the entire India in the process of not doing so. In fact, the five members of the Muslim League had joined the Interim Government only for forcing this division of India."

***

Nevertheless, Patel was not happy with India's division. Inwardly he felt its rancour for long like his Bapu did. It was quite clear even before this division that at least two third members of the provincial committees of the Congress were in favour of Sardar Patel getting chosen as the Prime Minister of India. However Gandhi Ji had other opinion. And in the Congress then, Bapu's opinion carried more weight than the majority of the members owing to Gandhi's personal influence. This difference created a dilemma for Patel. But eventually he succeeded in getting over it.

"Why do you always keep mum when the topic is raised?"

"It has become my habit."

"You have the support of 12 States with you!"

"Even if there be a 22 not only 12… I'd…"

"You know by your not doing what people like, you'll cause much harm to the country's interest?"

"But Jawahar is quite competent and deserving."

"However, a bit indecisive. He procrastinates his decision."

"But at last he comes with one."

"By then the damage is done."

"Count the damage before me, caused by Jawahar's indecisiveness."

"Oh…it is enough, Sardar! No sense in arguments with you."

"As you please."

"But history would never forgive you."

"Why! What is my fault?"

"You didn't do what you should have!"

"You have developed an expertise in finding fault in my actions."

"Will you join the Cabinet or remain a people's leader only?"

"Now you're being quite aggressive!"

"You know… What big job you have at hand?"

"What's that?"

"You have to unite this diverse country into one nation!"

"That will be done."

"Do you have any plans?"

"Not at hand but it shall be done. First some big problems have to be solved."

The condition of the country was far from satisfactory. On the August 15th, a public holiday was declared. Lord Mountbatten made Nehru, Patel and other Minister's take their oath of secrecy as the Ministers. It was Gandhi Ji's insistence that made Nehru the PM and Patel became the Deputy PM and the Home Minister. Patel was declared Deputy PM on 24th August 1957.

Although the transfer of power had taken place, the transfer of the population was still continuing. The Muslims avenged what happened with their brothers in India and the Hindus and Sikhs did exactly the same with the Muslims to keep the score even. Man had become a beast in that period. The situation in Delhi had become quite explosive because most of the Magistrates and the police personnel were Muslims while the majority of population was of the Hindus. Deeming to be having an upper hand the Muslims cast the first blow.

It was quite a strange situation: minority attacking majority expecting a helping hand from the law and order enforcing authority!

The Home Secretary asked the Home Minister, "Sir! What should we do?"

"I'm also thinking about it."

"The Muslim dominated police force is well armed."

"Like the Punjab Police, have they started siding with the aggressive rioters?"

"Yes! The news reports confirm your suspicion!"

"Sir," the orderly butted in, "the rioters are creating a havoc."

"We will soon do something. In a few days things will be better. We must get forces from outside. Ask for a Gorakha platoon."

The secretary immediately went to his desk to prepare such an order."

"Ask for army from the Bengal and M.P. also," said the Minister.

Although the action was taken immediately, still the disturbances could be controlled only after a month.

In the Punjab, things were becoming very disturbing. The Sikhs, getting the news of the massacre of their brothers in Lahore had their blood boiling with the fire of revenge.

Patel as the Home Minister, had a meeting with Master Tara Singh, the noted Sikh leader.

"Sardar, the Sikhs are getting mad with the fire of revenge."

"I know, Master Ji."

"Here the refugee's problem is confusing the situation all the more!"

"We must deal peacefully," the Home Minister suggested: "You must talk to your people."

Soon a meeting of the prominent Sikh leaders was arranged. Sardar had preliminary talks with them. And then he addressed a big Sikh rally on 30th Sept.

"I appeal to my Sikh brethrens that they must use their influence fully to establish peace. You can only salvage their feelings. I know how difficult it is to fight against all odds while separated from your dear ones! Remember that blood for blood leads only to gory violence. Allow the Muslims leaving this country a peaceful passage. Only then your brethren can expect safe passage to India. Also, I know that yours is a race of warriors. You must have your own squads of the volunteers to help the distressed here." And this way Sardar Patel tried to pacify the frayed tempers of the Sikhs. It did help in normalizing the conditions.

Now the question of funds arose. The Govt. didn't have adequate resources to arrange much funds.

Patel raised this issue in the Cabinet.

"We must establish a cell to create funds for the refugees."

However Nehru Ji had his misgivings about its proper use. But Patel said: "This is none of your concern. I will see to it. First we must have a head for getting money from various sources."

When the fund-head was created, they started getting enough funds. But Patel had to fight on the two fronts simultaneously: one the internal and the other was external. While he didn't mind facing the external problems the internal ones were really heart breaking.

One day just after breakfast he received the news about Gandhi Ji's 'Anshan' (no food till the demands are met).

"Why this Anshan against his own people? Now there is no British rule!"

"I don't comprehend his way of thinking," said an apparently irritated PM Nehru.

"What does he want?" Patel said in an exasperated tone.

"He wants the money due to Pakistan must be transferred immediately," Pt. Ji explained: "I don't want it to be held back either. But giving it immediately would make them use against only us. Their forces are advancing towards Kashmir."

"We can't give it to them to buy weapons and hurl them onto us only."

"No money to the aggressor," declared the PM, "This will be suicidal."

"Perhaps Bapu has the most humanistic approach."

"But now we have to run a country in these disturbing times. One has to be practical and worldliwise."

"But first you must arrange for Rs.55 crores to be given to Pakistan. This is what Bapu wants."

"I think this is what we can't avoid," Patel said. He was certainly not in favour of giving Pakistan this huge amount. Still he agreed.

In fact what was more rankling his heart was a kind of schism developing between his and Nehru's ways of thinking. Everyday they were having discussions on what to do and what not. He knew that Jawahar was more a visionary while he was much more practical. The clash between the visionary approach and practical reality was disturbing the administration in general.

One day Patel sought a private interview with Bapu:

"Come on Sardar, be seated," Gandhi Ji welcomed him affectionately.

"Bapu! I want to quit the Cabinet."

"Why? What happened?"

"Nothing… My health is failing."

"Sardar! You are too strong to be disturbed by such bouts of illness! I know you have growing differences with Jawahar. Shed off these pretention and come straight to the point."

"Bapu! You have many able persons to replace me. Then the administration will run smoothly."

"No, Sardar!" Gandhi Ji said with firmness. "Your and Jawahar's presence is necessary in the Cabinet for the sake of the country. And remember you are irreplaceable. We don't have any other Sardar."

"But, Bapu… please! I can't work in the present conditions…!"

"No… hold it… for some time. Now I'm getting late for my evening prayers. Then after I shall issue a statement to relieve you from your predicament."

But as they say, 'man proposes Gods disposes!' That statement from Bapu was never made! On that very day, that is 30th Jan. 1948, Gandhi Ji attained immortality! Nathuram Godse killed him.

Bapu's funeral procession was going. The 'Ramdhun' being played but Patel's feet were unsteady. He sat near the glowing body of his Bapu.

Now Bapu has quitted his mortal coil… now no one would do any 'Anshan', give instructions emerging from his conscience… no one would go to the prayer-meeting. All the Congressmen accompanying Bapu's last journey felt as though Bapu had expired but Patel had become a soul-less person. An unexpressed grief ever flitted across his face. He was acting like a zombie!

It was after Bapu's death that Patel could realize what Bapu was to him… his soul, his father, his friend – philosopher and guide!

One day his daughter Mani asked: "Why are you so forlorn?"

"Dear… I don't know. This grief is uncontrollable for me."

"But… one day everyone has to go this way!" Mani said.

"But he was not everyone. He was to me the very source of life."

"It was God's will, Sire!"

"How could God be so cruel to us?"

Mani informed him changing the topic: "Sire! Here is a good news! Dahya Bai is blessed with a son. You are grandpa now!"

"Oh… lovely!" Sardar's face radiated a warm glow!

Sardar was happy to take his grandson in his lap. His general demeanour became more cheerful. But it was just a passing phase. Internally he felt broken. Often he would keep on gazing at the sky in the night – as if searching for his Bapu's star!

Mani informed him that his medical check up was due. The doctor checked his pulse-rate and BP, saying:

"Sir! You must get out of the gloom. You have to be fit and well to strengthen this nation. You can't afford to be gloomy."

"Well, there are so many to do it. Bapu has trained many for this purpose."

"They could get us independence. But you have to unite this country into a strong nation. There are not many who could do so."

"No, Jawahar is there. I'm sure he will rise to the occasion."

Although medicines and psychological treatment given by the doctor continued, Sardar couldn't feel as strong as he used to feel. He had done enough… He was reminded of his activities during the past five months for uniting the country – his biggest achievement so far.

***

About six months ago, Sardar was quite worried about the sectionalism growing in the country. Mahadeva was sitting on the chair across the table littered with a variety of maps marked with red and blue pencils. He asked Patel: "Sardar what are you doing?"

"Beholding these marks on the body of our Bharat Mata!"

"What a poetic allegory, sir!"

"Also, Mahadeva! I see these bloody marks as well emerging out of the cut made on her body!"

"You seem to be still not reconciled to the division!"

"Not only the division; what pains me most is the manner it has been done in. Had it been the clear cut division, I'd have tolerated it. But it is not so. This country has no clear cut pockets of the Hindus and the Muslims. They have been living intermingled this way for centuries! Now the Muslims in the Hindu pockets and the vice-versa would give them much heart-burning because of the poison permeating the atmosphere in the free India.

"I hope with the passage of time, things will improve. But what have you decided about the princely states? The foreigners have given them freedom to join with India or Pakistan or even remain independent. It was surely the most heinous move on the part of the British! They wanted to weaken India."

"That I'd tackle," Sardar said with confidence. "I have a clear roadmap to achieve our destination."

"Have you heard the declaration made by the state of Travancore?"

"Even the Nizam of Hyderabad is taking somersault every day. But soon I'll find some solution. I have made the necessary moves."

Meanwhile, M.A. Jinnah was still hopeful of getting three more bordering states: Jodhpur, Jaisalmer and Bikaner apart from Junagarh and Nizam of Hyderabad.

Lord Mountbatten thought it to be a passing phase before the things falling into their grooves. But thede matters should have been decided prior to the transfer of power. On 13th June the Viceroy had summoned a conference which was attended from the Congress' side by Nehru, Patel and the then Congress President Acharya Kripalani and from the Muslim League by M.A. Jinnah, Liyaqat Ali, Abdul Rehman Nishtar and from the Sikhs' side Sardar Baldev Singh. In the capacity of the political advisor Sir Conrad Confield also attended it.

In the conference, Patel and Nehru opposed the freedom option for the Princely States while – as expected – Jinnah supported it. This led to a heated discussion and an impasse. At last the decision was taken to create a separate department to deal with the princely states' problem.

The job was entrusted to Viceroy's constitutional advisor, V.P. Menon who submitted his report by 25th June, 1947. By July this department had come into existence which was kept under Patel's control who chose Menon as its secretary.

On 5th July 1947 Sardar Patel issued a statement to all the States that according to the previous agreement, the central would deal with foreign affairs, defence and transport subjects. On 10th July the rulers of Patiala, Gwalior and many other states met Sardar Patel at the latter's residence in Delhi. They held wide ranging discussions.

Jinnah found this meeting of the States' rulers with Patel as injurious to his Pakistan's interest. He made it no secret and expressed his opposition to it in a public rally. But neglecting Jinnah's opposition many more states' rulers met Patel on 25th July again and showed their preference for Patel's decision in this matter.

Before that, on 15th July the Viceroy had also called a meeting of the 'Naresh Mandal' (an association of the heads of the princely states) and requested these rulers to entrust their foreign, defence and transporting affairs to India or Pakistan – whichever fell nearer to their boundaries. In this meeting a draft proposal for this purpose was also made with the consultation of the Viceroy.

On this agreement of merger of the princely states into the Indian Union all the princely rulers barring Hyderabad, Kashmir and Junagarh had signed without any problem. Then after, these state heads kept on meeting Sardar Patel, his secretary V.P. Menon and the Viceroy, Mountbatten as and when they wanted.

For M.A. Jinnah, this was a very trying phase as he wanted most princely states merging with Pakistan. It was on his assurances that some states were dilly-dallying. Later on, these were also agreed for their merger with India after Sardar created such conditions for them. It was also agreed that these princely states' agreements with the British Raj would also be honoured by the Indian Union with necessary modifications.

But these problems and others kept on emerging immediately after India's independence. Although the

Tricolour began to flutter from the Red Fort of Delhi and all the British impact began to get diffused right from the President's House to the Parliament, peace was still far away. Patel was still apprehensive of the brewing of many more disturbances.

And eventually that happened for which Patel was quite apprehensive!

***

Sardar was quietly walking in the verandah of his residence in Delhi. He had been receiving news of disturbance from every quarter. And wherever the disturbance arose, it was he who was called to do the needful. He found that both Bhoola Bhai and Mahadeva Bhai approaching towards his room.

"Good Morning, Sardar!"

"There is nothing 'good' around, Mahadeva! Anyway what brings you here so early?"

"Things are not peaceful in Orissa and M.P. interior areas, particularly in the tiny princedoms!"

"Yes! I have heard the news. Nilgiri is also quite restive. I'm making the ruling heads to sign the agreement of merger with Indian Union. I know that these princes would have to be offered a bait in the form of the Privy Purse! That provision has been made."

"Well, Sardar! We're glad you are here," Bhoola Bhai said, "else the things would have remain suspended in the indecisiveness," he said casting an oblique comment on the current PM's way of working.

"Well," Sardar said with a smile. "He has more time in this world. I don't have that much."

Sardar Patel was awfully busy in ensuring the merger of the princely states. He had an able support in the form of his secretary, Mr. Menon. Both would use all kinds of methods to have the princes toe with their line. Most of the princes were worried owing to their losing their control over their estates financially. They would invariably question Sardar: "How can we maintain our status following the merger?" Sardar also knew that if they are assured of financial security and the partial upkeep of their erstwhile honour, most of them would accept the merger. Sardar would in some cases – like in Junagarh – make the people revolt against their rulers. His strategy was to get these princes cornered by their own subjects. In Junagarh he made such conditions, that its Nawab had to flee to Pakistan alone and his state was duly merged in Saurashtra.

In fact, merger of the state of Nizam, Hyderabad Merged as the biggest hurdle in the process of India's unification. The Nizamshahi was the state carved out of the Mughal Empire in the 18th Century. It was in 1713 that the Mughal ruler Farrukhseer appointed Mir Kamurddin as the ruler of Hyderabad with the title Nizam-ul-mulk. Although this state deemed itself to be a part of the Mughal Empire till 1857 when Bhadur Shah Zafar – the last Mughal Emperor – was dethroned, for all practical purpose it was an independent state. Since its rulers had not to fight any major battle, this state continued to prasper and gather wealth. At the time of India's independence, its ruler the Nizam was supposed to be the richest individual in the entire Asia.

Sardar had to deal with the Hyderabad state quite cautiously. He was studying thoroughly its historic and geographic situations. When Menon came to him with a lot of files, Patel was busy reading certain historical documents.

Menon: "Sir! Nizam had tried to remain aloof from the local influence. He encouraged Urdu despite Kannad, Telugu and Marathi being the lingua franca of the region. He even didn't allow Bombay, Madras railway line to pass through his state."

Patel knew that in 1946 when the provincial assembly was constituted, among its total 122 members, Muslims were as high as 71 whereas 85% of the population of the Hyderabad region was of Hindus. And when Indian Independence Act was declared, the Nizam announced that he would not send his states' representations either to Indian Constituent Assembly or even for that of Pakistan. Not only that, he announced that on 15th August 1947 he would also declare his state's independence. However, deeming that to be an impossible option, he sent a special delegation under the chairmanship of Nawab Chhataari on 11th July 1947 to negotiate with the Govt. This delegation met many officials in Delhi but scrupulously avoided meeting Sardar, for it knew that Sardar would make them sign the agreement for the merger!

But Patel was quite aware of these movements in Delhi. He was already getting information about Hyderabad from his sources which included Mahadeva Shastri and his own secretary, Mr. Menon. They had a detailed exchange of notes the following way:

Shastri: "A communal organization called 'Ittehadul Ameen' has been created in Hyderabad."

Patel: "The same whose leader is Sayyad Quasid Rijvi?"

Shastri: "Yes!"

Menon: "These group members are called the Razakaar."

Shastri: "The Hyderabad papers are also fanning up this kind of communal passion. One of them has published a scathing criticism of the Central Govt.'s pronounced pro-Hindu role."

Menon: "The Nizam's adviser is an Englishmen, called Walton Matcan. He has suggested some modified conditions for the State's merger with India."

Patel: "I won't accept any such thing. The merger's conditions will be determined by the people's wish and not by the Nizam's whims."

Menon: "A new delegation has come from Hyderabad led by Ali Yavar Jung! He claims that if Hyderabad state is forcibly merged with the Indian Union, the Muslim population would stage a massive revolt violently."

Patel: "What was Mountbatten's reaction to this threat."

Menon: "He conveyed his reaction in strong terms that the Govt. won't keep quiet either if the law and order situation is disturbed."

Patel: "He is a wise-man."

Shastri: "What are you planning, Patel Saheb?"

Patel: "At present observing the reaction of the so-called secular persons! I'd plan after my full assessment of the situation. But, it is heard that Jinnah has also ditched Nizam."

Menon: "Nizam was willing to buy some deadly weapons from abroad with a huge seem and he wanted

Jinnah's help. But Jinnah never wanted his any involvement in an international conspiracy."

Patel: "Menon! You should now draft a proposal from our side which should be a bit liberal. We shouldn't let him get any opportunity to escape away from us."

Patel's tactics worked and Nizam agreed to enter into a pact with the Indian origin.

Mahadeva Shastri opined: "Now this act has made Nizam come down a bit from his lofty stand."

Menon: "He did have prolonged consultations with Kasmi Rizvi."

Shsastri: "In fact all his erstwhile advisers have resigned."

Menon: "They all learnt about your unhappiness with their stand."

Patel: "Good! Now he has appointed Layak Ali instead."

Menon: "We must start afresh to deal with him and prepare a fresh agreement."

The draft was also shown to Mountbatten and he too agreed that it could be made into a good proposal. In order to become a ruler with sovereign rights, the Nizam agreed to part with some of his previous prerogatives. He agreed to sign the instrument of accession before the expiry of this new agreement. In return the Govt. of India would honour its previous commitments with the State of Hyderabad.

The Nizam had also written a letter to the Viceroy promising his State's no merger with Pakistan and in the event of India and Pakistan getting engaged in an armed confrontation, it would remain neutral!

Sardar Patel, on 29th Nov. 1947, informed the Indian Constituent Assembly about this agreement. From India's side Kannaiya Lal Maniklal Munshi was appointed as India's Agent General in Hyderabad. After a few days, Nizam promulgated two ordinances: one, India's no valuable metals will be exported, and second, the Indian currency won't be acceptable in Hyderabad State! The Govt. of India demanded explanation from the Nizam as both these ordinances ran counter to its interest. But Nizam continued to dilly-dally with the explanation as he wanted to evade this issue. But the reason for this dilly-dallying was revealed in a couple of days, which also exposed Nizam's double game. The Nizam had loaned out securities worth Rupees twenty crores to Pakistan and he has also appointed its exclusive public relations man in Pakistan.

On 30th Jan. 1948 a delegation led by Nawab Moin and Nawab Juing reached Delhi from Hyderabad with the complaint that the Indian newspapers were making a vicious propaganda against the Hyderabad State and the Nizam was not allowed to sell away his costly weapons. Since Nizam's double game with Pakistan was on, he was making a series of allegations on the Govt. of India.

These confusions, deliberately created, caused Razakaar's attacks on innocent Hindus. The Nizam turned a blind eye towards these happenings. But the Govt. of India couldn't have neglected these events. The people of India were going quite restless and the majority of the population wanted the Govt.'s intervention immediately.

As the bad luck would have it, it is amidst these turbulences that Gandhi Ji was murdered. The Govt.'s hands were tied for sometime. Meanwhile, Kasim Ali began to openly puke venom against Hindus. While his organization was instigating the Muslims to attack Hindu in the garb of the Razakaars, Kasim Ali encouraged these Razakaars by calling them as 'the saviours' of the victimized Muslims!

The Razakaars' these violent activities were provoking other communities in the rest of the country. At last on 21st Feb, a meeting of the CMs of Madras, Bombay and M.P. was called whose Chairman was Sardar Patel. In this meeting the turbulent conditions all over the country were discussed and their possible solutions were charted out.

About a fortnight after this meeting as the representatives of the Nizam – Sir Walter Matcan, Layak Ali and Nawab Moin Jung – came to Delhi, they were asked to spell out the conditions in Hyderabad. But Layak Ali became aggressive to say: "Razakaars don't attack anyone; they only save the poor Muslims when they are attacked by the majority communities." Later on, he also emphasized: "Unless the Indian Union enters a formal agreement with Hyderabad, the 20 crores' securities given to Pakistan won't be taken back."

However, Lord Mountbatten warned him: "Sardar Patel says that unless the conditions are normalized, nothing will be done." But while a common communiqué was drafted to be released soon, the heart attack suffered by Sardar Patel delayed all such activities.

On 20th March V.P. Menon wrote a letter to Layak Ali in which explanation was called as to why Hyderabad violated its agreement with Indian Union. When this letter was delivered to him through the office of K.M. Munshi, the Agent General, Layak Ali had the temerity to reply: "The Nizam won't grudge a martyr's death and millions of Muslims will follow his glorious path!" The threat enshrined was quite apparent. It was like the kettle calling the pot black!

In fact these Razakaars had convinced the Nizam that the latter would get the support of all the Muslims the world-over if India dare attach them. They knew that even if there be an economic blockade enforced by India over their land-locked state, they had enough resources to last for at least six months. They would also supply weapons to the gullible Muslims. Layak Ali was also in correspondence with Pt. Nehru in whom he detected a streak of sympathy for the Muslims.

On 8th April when Lord Mountbatten asked Nizam to stop Layak Ali from giving provocative speeches, Ali again wrote to Nehru to convince him that nothing of the sort was happening. Nehru asked him to meet Patel to clarify his position. At last when he confronted Patel, Patel asked him: "I have heard your saying that should the Indian Army dare attack Hyderabad, they would first find the bones of more than one and half crore Hindus! I advise you not to flare up communal passion if you want your and your Nizam's welfare." Then giving a stern warning, the Home Minister said: "Understand this that Hyderabad State's problem will be solved like it was solved in the cases of other princely states. We won't let Hyderabad disturb our federal set up we created after much sweat and toil. We shall not spare any means or method to maintain peace in your province."

Layak Ali felt pulverized with Patel's clear cut warning. V.P. Menon was also there in the meeting. At Patel's advice he drew up four proposals for getting Nizam's consent. These, in nut-shell, were:

- Ban all Razakaar activities and their demonstrations/ rallies.
- Release all the Congressmen imprisoned in Hyderabad State.
- The present set up of the State's Constitution must be modified to allow representation of all the communities.
- For this purpose a Constituent Council should be constituted within the period of maximum one year.

But before these could be implemented a Bombay-Madras train was attached by the Razakaars, killing some and wounding many, at Hyderabad's suburban station, Ganga Nagar. Despite the presence of the Hyderabad Police, it remained to be an observer only. In fact with the help of the local police, the Razakaars became more aggressive. Even the Christians and Jews were also victimized. Not only that it was also learnt by the local intelligence that one Pakistan protected weapon dealer from Australia – Sydney Cotton was supplying weapons to the Razakaars. But despite these disturbing news items Pt. Nehru was still against the military action. Once in a Cabinet Meeting Patel had even resigned. Later on, he was requested by the then Governor General, C. Rajgopalachari and he withdrew it. He was reminded of Gandhi Ji's last words: "Vallabh! Think of the country!" He knew that unless the military action was taken, Hyderabad problem would disturb the map of the South India rather irreparably! Finally, he decided the day for the military action – 13th Dec. 1948. At that time the Chief of Staff of the Indian Army was General Blushair. This Englishman's psychology was against doing the action on 13th. He asked the Home Minister (Patel):

"Shouldn't we postpone the action by a day – to 14th Dec.?"

Patel knew that things might worsen further in twenty four hours. So he said: "No! 13th is okay. We the Gujaratis deem it as an auspicious number!"

"But, Sir!" argued the General: "Many others also call 13th to be rather inauspicious number."

"No problem," Patel suggested: "Why not do the action on 12th Dec. itself! They say the earlier the better – particularly for an auspicious work!"

And despite Pt. Nehru's unwillingness, the Military Action was taken on 12th with a two pronged attack: one from Sholapur-Hyderabad route and the other from Bejavad-Hyderabad passage. Leading the first prong, General J. N. Chaudhary eliminated 800 Razakaars. Their boasting of possessing the special weapons couldn't check the Indian forces grin. After just two days' armed confrontation everything became normal. The Indian forces kept on advancing and on 17th Dec. 1948 the Hyderabad force's Commander-in-Chief L. A. Rousse surrendered before General Chaudhari. All the Hyderabad State's Ministers including Layak Ali were put under house arrest. General Chaudhari was appointed the Military Governor of Hyderabad.

On 19th Dec. the leader of the Razakaar, Kasim Rizvi was arrested. The application given earlier by the Nizam to take the Hyderabad issue to the UNO was subsequently withdrawn through a telegraphic message.

The people of Hyderabad wanted Nizam dethroned immediately but Sardar avoided any haste in these matters. Although all the ministers of the erstwhile Hyderabad State were under the house arrest, Layak Ali managed to slip into Pakistan. Even though he was a deserter, his property was not forfeited. Later on his property (or the worth of it) was sent to him in Pakistan. Who helped him flee to Pakistan and why his property was so casually transferred and not entrusted to the Waqf Board are still some mysterious questions, with no apparently convincing answers.

It was in Feb. 1949 that Sardar Patel reached Hyderabad. The Nizam had himself come to the airport, hand-bound in utter submission. Patel greeted him magnanimously. As has been his nature he had never been vindictive. He arranged for the Nizam's comfortable stay in Hyderabad like he had done for other rulers' stay in their own erstwhile kingdoms.

***

Patel was quite perturbed inwardly with his differences with the PM Pt. Nehru with the passage of time. Had he been not bound with his pledge to Gandhi Ji, he might have resigned much before. Even once he did so but Rajgopalachari and other stalwarts forced him to continue in the Cabinet. They all knew that Pt. Nehru was quite competent and honest, but he was move a visionary and not a practical man as the leader of India in those turbulent time should have been. It was only Patel who could fill up that deficiency. Pehaps Gandhi Ji also knew it and hence his insistence was on Patel for not leaving the Cabinet.

Even before the Hyderabad issue could be settled, Pakistan forces in the garb of the Primitive Kabaiali class began to infiltrate into Kashmir. The ruler of Jammu and Kashmir had come to Delhi following the infiltration. Since Kashmir struck an emotional chord in Pt. Nehru's heart –

his clan's original dwelling place – the PM decided to keep this matter in his fold only, though like all other princely states, this issue ought to have been also given to the Home Minister.

Nehru's adamance fanned by Sheikh Abdullah's ambition had complicated the matters in Kashmir's merger.

Patel never deemed Sheikh Abdullah a reliable person who was then the PM of Kashmir. Patel had warned Gandhi Ji also about it. The large area of Kashmir which had fallen under Kabailis' control should have been subjected to the military action according to Patel, but Nehru let this issue be taken to the UNO as suggested by Sheikh Abdullah. At that time, too, many stalwarts had warned Nehru about escalating this Kashmir problem to no end. Sardar Patel had himself told one of his confidant, who became the Congress President later on that: "Give me just 15 days time and this Kashmir problem will be settled once forever!" He never wanted any special constitutional provision – like the Article 370 – for this State. Once the ruler of Kashmir had merged his state with the Indian Union, why should there be a special status for it? The Kashmir issue is still hanging fire.

In fact not only these states' merger but some other princely states' confluence with the Indian Union created much problem for our country. But Patel's iron-hand achieved the needful. Given below is the list of the merger of as many as 522 princely states with Indian Union covering as much as about 4 lakh square miles area, with broad details:

The Princely States that Merged with the Indian Union

Erstwhile Names of the States	Province they Merged into	Area in Sq. Miles	Date of the Merger
222 states of Gujarat and Saurashtra like Junagarh etc.	Saurashtra	21062	15th Feb 1948
18 states of Rajasthan like Jodhpur & Jaipur etc.	Rajasthan Federation	128424	7th April 1948
Gwalior, Indore and other 35 States of Madhya Pradesh	Madhya Bharat	46710	15th June 1948
8 states of Punjab like Kapurthala, Patiala, Maler-kotla, Nabha, Easter Faridkot, Jeend, Jalagarh, Kalasia etc.	Patiala	10090	30th Aug 1948
Travancore & Cochin	Travancore	9155	1st July 1949
Anjagarh and other States of Orissa	Orissa	23637	1st Jan. 1948
Bastar and 14 other States	Madhya Pradesh	31598	1st Jan. 1948
Makarai	Madhya Pradesh	151	2nd Feb. 1948
Loha	Eastern Punjab	226	23rd Feb. 1948
Bagana Palle	Madras	259	3rd March 1948
Puddukkottai	Madras	1185	3rd March 1948
Dujana	Eastern Punjab	92	3rd March 1948
Aundha, Alakkot etc. 17 States	Bombay	7651	8th March 1948
Pataudi	Eastern Punjab	53	7th April 1948
144 Small States of Gujarat	Bombay	17680	10th June 1948
Kharasawan & Saraivela	Bihar	623	18th May 1948
Mayurbhanja	Orissa	4034	1st Jan. 1949
Sirohi	Bombay	6994	5th Jan. 1949
Kolhapur	Bombay	3219	1st March 1949
Baroda	Bombay	8236	1st May 1949
Sandoor	Madras	158	11th May 1949
Tehri Garhwal	U.P.	4516	1st Aug. 1949
Benaras	U.P.	466	5th Oct.1949
Rampur	U.P.	894	1st Jan. 1950
Koocha Bihar	Western Bengal	1321	1st Jan. 1950
21 Eastern States of Punjab	Himachal	10500	15th April 1948
Kuchcha	Gujarat	8461	1st June 1948
Bhopal	M.P.	6921	1st June 1949
Tripura	Tripura (Assam)	8620	15th Oct. 1949
Orchha, Ajaygarh & other 35 States	Vindhya Pradesh	24600	1st Oct. 1950

It is quite clear from the above list that how hectic would have been the period for Sardar Patel between 15th August 1947 and 15th December 1950. Apart from ensuring the smooth merger of the 522 princely states into the Union of India he had to discharge his duties in the absence of the PM since he has also the Deputy PM. When on 7th Oct. 1949 Pt. Nehru went to visit US, Canada, England and other European countries, Patel discharged his very cumbersome duties as financially the prices were soaring up. Apart from that he had also to look after the consolidation of the ranks and wages in all the All India Services including the erstwhile ICS.

***

One evening Sardar Patel was relaxing at his Govt. bungalow and he thought of Gandhi Ji. Manibhen had been telling him that he must start something solid and everlasting in the memory of Gandhi Ji.

"What should be done?"

"You must create a Gandhi Memorial Fund so that with that the nation could do something to fulfill the dreams Bapu had seen for our nation!"

"Yes, a nice idea," said Patel. He thought "Now I have something to look forward to."

"Okay! Call Shri Birla Ji and other industrialists from Bombay." Getting the hint those nationalist industrialists quickly came to Patel.

Patel said: "I want a 'Gandhi Memorial Fund' be established soon. I expect an initial contribution from all of you."

Ghanshyam Das Birla Ji assured him: "you don't worry for money collection. We will have our Bapu's wishes fulfilled.

After a few days some priests came from Somnath, the religious shrine on the coast of Gujarat. They wanted their famous temple to be repaired. Sardar Patel asked them to wait for some days.

In the meantime he consulted some experts in the archaeological department and summoned the renowned scholar and administrator, K.M. Munshi, to his chamber.

"Munshi Ji! I have learned from the archaeological experts that the Somnath Temple needs urgent repairs. I want you to become the adviser of the Temple Repair Committee and have the temple repaired with such a class that its old glory could be justified."

Mr. K.M. Munshi gladly accepted the job. Soon the work began and within a year the grand Somnath Temple stood at the place of its dilapidated version. The work of consecrating the Idol inside was accomplished by no one else but India's first President Dr. Rajendra Prasad.

Patel never felt any hitch in doing anything which he thought to be just and proper. He was an out and out secularist and had there been any (religious) dilapidated and renowned shrine of some other faith, he would have promptly come forward to get it repaired. For him secularism was not to be shown to public, it was to be practised in one's heart.

People had started recognizing his abilities and all the big universities were vying with each other to honour him. While on 3rd November 1948 Nagpur University conferred the honourary degree of 'Doctor of Laws', the Benaras Hindu University and the University of Allahabad conferred him the same degrees soon after. In fact many educational, social and cultural organization wanted to call him to honour him, but Sardar had no time. Tackling the internal problems of the country, ensuring the smooth transfer of power within the country, smoothening the All India Services and consolidating the law and order situation made him work non-stop and strenuously. With the result, his health began to deteriorate fast. Even though Mani and Dahya repeatedly requested him to relax, he couldn't. Once he went to Moussorie (the hill station in U.P.) but the problem of the Hyderabad merger quickly brought him back to Delhi. Sardar Patel had also started feeling quite indifferent with these worldly activities.

***

In December 1950 he had to go to Bombay on some urgent work. Knowing his condition, Manibhen accompanied him. Although she wanted him not to travel anymore, Sardar didn't agree. In fact he had been feeling a kind of pain in the left side of his heart whenever he exerted physically. The doctors in Delhi had advised him total rest but how could a dedicated person ever think of postponing his work owing to any personal discomfiture? At last he went to Bombay.

Bombay had been his arena for many personal and official activities. While he was lying in his bed, Manibhen came there with a glass of medicated milk as advised by the doctor. His one close friend was also near him at that time. While lying on the bed he had dictated a letter to his steno. When the steno left, he said to his friend:

"My dear! This frail canoe is now unable to float on this sea of worldly existence."

"What are you saying Sardar? Don't even think so. You are our strength."

"The fact is that I feel my soul needs rest. I want to be near my Bapu."

"Sir! You're forgetting your words to your Bapu! The country's boat is still not stable."

"There are other capable oarsmen to guide it. I have done my bit."

When Mani reached there and heard these talks, she got a shock. She had never heard his father speak so despondently.

"Please don't talk much and have this medicated milk. It will make you sleep!" Manibhen said to her father.

"Sleep I want dear --- a long one," and saying so Sardar drank the milk.

Then while lying quietly he felt as if a panorama of his past life was parading before him:

"Koel baithee hai…" he felt as though his wife was humming her favourite song… She seemed to be saying, "You must drink this milk and eat these snacks… these have been cooked by me.."

Sardar felt as if he was in hallucination. When he opened his eyes, he found none in the room. Again turning side he tried to sleep.

"Sardar!" He felt as if his Bapu (Gandhi Ji) was speaking with his lisping accent. "Have courage, Jawahar admires your courage. Have trust in him. But remember his visionary imagination needs your practical approach… Don't feel exhausted. Come and sing with me: "Vaishnav Jan to tene Kahihiye…"

Sardar again opened his eyes. But he found Mani sitting closely on a chair, reading something. "Go and sleep my dear! It is okay with me."

As he said so he felt a sharp and throbbing pain emerging from almost the middle of his chest and traversing towards the left arm. "Oh! I'm feeling an excruciating pain! It's suffocating me!"

Mani was nervous. She immediately called the doctor attending her father. Immediately the ambulance was called to shift him to the hospital fitted with an ICU.

But before the Iron-Man could be taken there, the valiant, brave Sardar succumbed to that pain and quitted his mortal coil!

***

The news of Sardar's death spread like a wildfire plunging the whole country into the depth of sorrow. 31st Oct. 1950 was indeed a bad day for the country. The news of his sad demise was given to the Parliament at 11:30 a.m. next morning. Immediately the President, Dr. Rajendra Prasad and the Prime Minister, Pt. Nehru left for Bombay. Mr. Gadgil at that time was in Poona. The Congress head also rushed to Bombay. Pt. Nehru had earlier advised Sardar before his trip to Bombay that he must stay in Delhi. But as was his nature, Sardar could not be distracted from his chosen decision.

The news of Sardar's demise made the Chief Ministers of many Indian States, even some erstwhile rulers rush to Bombay.

But a kind of political game commenced even then. While the people in general wanted Sardar to be cremated at Chaupati – a huge ground on the sea-shore – the Bombay administration was against it. It was at Chaupati that Lokmanya Gangadhar Tilak was cremated. It was believed that the then Chief Minister of Bombay, B.G. Kher, didn't want Sardar Patel to be offered that honour which the people of Bombay had shown for Tilak. Hence he advised the then Home Minister of Bombay, Mr. Morarji Desai, to ensure no cremation at Chaupati on the plea that it was difficult to ensure all security arrangement there in short time. His argument was that it was impossible to make the arrangement for the state funeral at such a short notice.

This issue created some tension in the grief-stricken atmosphere also. When Sardar Patel's younger brother and son were asked to give their choice for cremation, they said: "Cremate him where the people want." People wanted the cremation at Chaupati. At last the Home Minister of Bombay decided to go by the people's choice. The time fixed was 5 p.m. But the decision was declared when very little time was left for the cremation. The Army Contingent expressed its inability to make the needed arrangement at such a short notice, although a senior police official had told a section of the crowd: "Things can be arranged in just 15 minutes time."

Nevertheless, the concerned people thought it better to create no scene and accept what Mr. Desai and Mr. Kher said. Eventually it was decided to do the cremation at the Queen's Road Crematorium.

The funeral procession departed from the house at 5:20 p.m. Just a few yards away from the crematorium, the body was taken off the carriage and many leaders carried it on their shoulders to the real point. Sardar's body was laid on a raised platform where PM Nehru, Sir Maharaj Singh the then Governor of Bombay), Maharaja Bhavnagar (the then Governor of Madras), Pt. Govind Ballabh Pant and other top leaders touched reverentially the feet of the body. Govind Ballabh Pant has become so emotionally broken that he couldn't hide his tears. Pt. Nehru personally came to him to help him retain his composure.

Exactly at 7:40 p.m. Sardar Patel's body was laid on the pyre and his son Dahyabhai Patel gave it the 'Mukhagni' (lit up with the body with fire amidst chanting of holy hymns). And that great Iron Man of India, Sardar Patel, had his body consumed by the raging fire. The glow of the fire reminded many present there of the great radiance that his face used to shed even while passing though the most turbulent period.

The shifting of the venue of his cremation remained for many days a burning topic for the various national newspapers. At last Manibhen had to make her public statement that it was her father's wish that he be cremated at the Queens Road Crematorium, where the cremation of her mother (Sardar Patel's wife, Jhaverba) and her uncle (Sardar Patel's elder brother, Vitthal Bhai) were also done. Many claimed that Manibhen was pressurized to make such a public statement. However, the truth remains that many controversies regarding Sardar Patel and Nehru's mutual bickerings still remain an occasional topic of the country's so-called investigative journalism. Nevertheless the truth can't be gainsaid either that both were the great leaders of India.

Appendix -1

Tributes from the Great Leaders to Sardar Patel

We and our country know well about the great story of this great leader. History bears testimony to this fact that he was one of the great builders of our new India. Perhaps many of us would call him a great commander in our struggle for India's freedom. During the struggle he gave us solid guidance. In fact he was our tower of strength.

– Pt. Jawahar Lal Nehru

No praise of Sardar Patel can truly encompass his personality's all aspects. Nothing could obstruct his way ever, and no person or thought could distract him from his chosen path. He had a singular aim: India's freedom and India's prosperity. His was a truly awakened personality endowed with indomitable will, dedication for public service. With all these qualities he has left an indelible imprint on the creation of our new India.

– Pt. Govind Ballabh Pant

Sardar Patel was a unique personality among our top leaders. His leadership qualities gave rise to unity and feeling of bonhomie in our struggle for freedom. His name shall ever be remembered with honour by our generations.

– K. Hanumantaiyya

Sardar Saheb was truly the Iron-Man of our nation, having all the human qualities with magnanimity. During the period of national crises his indomitable will showed as a new direction for relief.

– J. D. Tapase

This great son of India was an organizer par-excellence, a great administrator and endowed with all leadership qualities. He was a stalwart in his own right – a Maharathi! In all the movements for India's freedom he appeared as the front-row fighter. Following India's independence, it was his leadership, indomitable will and inexhaustible courage that guided India to its glorious destiny. His greatest achievement in the context of national strength was his unification of India.

– Y. B. Chauhan

Mahatma Gandhi's assassination had petrified India with grief. India then appeared to be unprotected but his able disciples guided it. Sardar Patel's death has also given it a similar damage as he was the most faithful follower of Gandhi Ji who never turned back while waging the struggle for our freedom.

– Mohd. Kareem Chhagla

As we realize the importance of the Independence that we attained, we shall also find the honour for Sardar Patel in our hearts increasing tremendously. Right from 1916-17 to Gandhi's last days, every movement launched by Bapu had a very significant role of Sardar Patel. It would be very apt to say that all the programmes and big movements that Gandhi Ji launched were truly and faithfully implemented by Sardar Patel. Gandhi Ji had immense faith in Sardar's wisdom as he did nothing without his prior consultation with the latter. Not only that, at times when Sardar Patel's views differed with those of Gandhi Ji's, once the decision was taken Sardar would follow him quite devotedly. One can't even assess the shock that Sardar Patel felt by Gandhi Ji's death. He tried his level best to complete all the projects started by Gandhi Ji and never flinched from doing so till his last breath. Whatever Sardar Patel did in the last phase of his life can be well appreciated by all. We have no such example in our history of anyone achieving such a big laurel by uniting and merging so many princely states with our Indian Union. I don't think history of any other country in the world has any such example either.

– Babu Rajindra Prasad

Sardar Vallabh Bhai Patel, our 'Sardar Ji' was the most important leader in the Congress who under Gandhi Ji's able leadership laid the foundation of a new and independent India. With his iron-will he had become the life and soul of the Congress Party. It was his incomparable prudence and bold character that rightly gave him the epithet: "The Iron-Man". He never flinched from calling a spade a spade, no matter what the condition be. The Independence that India gained after a long struggle had his very vital role as well... He never said die... Before his death he could see the auspicious results of his efforts in the form of India's independence. He and other leaders could see the culmination of their cherished dream for which they suffered tortures and waged struggles. Sardar Patel's death is an irrepairable loss for India.

– Vivekananda Mukherji

The relation between Ram and Lakshman was truly reflected in the relationship between Mahatma Gandhi and Vallabh Bhai Patel. Those well versed with Ram's story can easily understand the depths of this relationship. Then nothing remains to be said about them. Vallabh Bhai had fought for very long for India, only if he could have survived a little longer!

– Chakravarti Rajgopalachari

It was my sheer good luck that I could get Sardar Vallabh Bhai like companion. I was aware of his unique spirit of bravery but I could stay with him only for 16 months… I can never forget his contribution for the welfare of Bardoli farmers.

– Mahatma Gandhi

Among his contemporaries Sardar Patel had a distinct role. In Indian history his name will remain immortally mentioned.

– Atlee

Before going to India in March 1947 I was not familiar with Sardar Patel's name. I was warned that this man was by nature adamant and had iron-will and it was difficult to elicit cooperation from him. But soon I was to learn that he was a man of magnanimous nature – ever friendly, full of human considerations and a very loveable person.

– Lord Mount-batten

Appendix - 2

Important Events of Sardar Patel's Life

Event	Year
➢ Birth	31st Oct. 1875
➢ Marriage	1893
➢ Passed Matriculation Exam.	1897
➢ 'Mukhtari' Practice beginning	1900
➢ Birth of the Daughter (Manibhen)	April 1903
➢ Birth of the Son (Dahya Bhai)	Nov 1905
➢ Death of Wife (Jhaverba)	11th Jan. 1909
➢ To England for the Bar-at-law Course	1910
➢ First Contact with Gandhi Ji and attending the Lucknow Congress	1916
➢ Kheda Satyagraha and becoming a Member of Ahmedabad Municipality	1917
➢ Soldier Recruitment Job being associated with Gandhiji	1918
➢ Publication of the Satyagraha Magazine without the permission	April 1919
➢ Decision to Establish Gujarat Vidyapeeth	July 1920
➢ Becoming the Chairperson of the Welcome Committee of Ahmedabad Congress	1921
➢ Jhanda Satyagraha	9th Sept. 1923
➢ Borsad Satyagraha	December 1923
➢ Becoming the Chairman of Ahmedabad's Municipality	1924
➢ Flood Relief in Gujarat as the Municipal Chairperson	1927
➢ Bardoli Satyagraha and Participation in the Calcutta Congress	1928
➢ Working Congress President	1930

First Imprisonment	March 1930
Second Imprisonment	August 1930
Third Imprisonment	December 1930
Becoming the President in Karachi Congress	March 1931
Imprisonment in the Yervada Jail	4th Jan. 1932
Release from the Jail owing to Poor Health	14th July 1934
Becoming Chairman of the Congress Parliamentary Board	1934
Serving the Plague Victims	March 1935
Participation in the Haripura Congress	1938
Imprisoned in the Civil Disobedient Movement	18th Nov. 1940
Released from Jail due to illness	20th Aug 1941
British – Quit India Proposal	April 1942
Imprisoned in the Ahmednagar Prison	9th August 1942
Release from the Imprisonment	15th June 1945
In the Shimla Conference	1945
Attempt to bring peace in the Naval Force's Rebellion	23rd Feb 1946
Talks with the Cabinet Mission	24th June 1946
Member of the Interim Govt.	2nd Sept. 1946
First time in the Constituent Assembly	9th Dec. 1946
Inaugurating the Vitthal Bhai Mahavidyalaya	4th April 1947
Appealing to all the Princely States for their merger with the Indian Union	5th July 1947
As the Home Minister and Deputy Prime Minister of India	15th August 1947
Addressing the Sikhs of Amritsar on Non-Violence	30th Sept. 1947
Getting Control on the Junagarh State	9th Nov. 1947
Resolved to have the Somnath Temple duly repaired	13th Nov. 1947

➢	Signing on the Instrument of Accession on behalf of the Indian Union merging 23 states of Orissa	14th Nov. 1947
➢	Inauguration of the Saurashtra Rajya Sangh	15th Feb. 1948
➢	Consent given for the merger of Indore-Gwalior States and other princely kingdoms	20-22 April 1948
➢	Consultation with the Industrialists for establishing 'Gandhi Smarak Nidhi'	May 1948
➢	Creation of 'Patiala - Punjab Rajya Sangh'	15th July 1948
➢	Order given for the Military Action in Hyderabad	12th Dec. 1948
➢	Meeting the Nizam in Hyderabad	24th Feb. 1949
➢	As the Acting Prime Minister	7th Oct-15th Nov1949
➢	As the Treasurer of Congress	16th Oct. 1950
➢	Departure to Bombay for Treatment	12th Dec. 1950
➢	Death	15th Dec. 1950

❑❑❑